Driving My Scooter ~
Through The Asteroid Field
Coming Down Over Venus
"Hallo Baba"

Sunny Jetsun

<u>S</u>he sent Shivas down my Spine

'She began to talk of her experiences in roaming about the world. When she talked about her wanderings she seemed to paint them: everything she described remained in my head like finished canvases by a master. We began by talking about China and the Chinese language which she had begun to study. Soon we were in North Africa, in the desert among peoples I had never heard of before. And then suddenly she was all alone, walking beside a river and the light was intense and I was following her as best I could in the blinding sun, but she got lost and I found myself wandering about in a strange land listening to a language I had never heard before. She is an artist of some sort because nobody has ever given me as she did the ambiance of a world of light such as I had never dreamed of and never hoped to see.'
Arrangement: 'The Colossus of Maroussi' Henry Miller
*

*for Raphaella ~ Sparkling Stars in her eyes and heart *

Looking for the Love ~ we are the Love

Driving My Scooter Through The Asteroid Field
Coming Down Over Venus ~ "Hallo Baba"

Sunny Jetsun

<u>**Books by the Same Author:**</u>
*'Light love * Angels from Heaven*
New Generation, Inspiration, Revolution, Revelation
All the Colours of Cosmic Rainbows'
*'Green Eve * Don't lose the Light Vortex **
My brain's gone on holiday ~ free flowing feelings'
'Surfing or Suffering ~ together * Sense Consciousness
fields of a body with streams and stars of hearts'
"When You're happy you got wings on your back ~
Reposez vos oreilles à Goa; We're only one kiss away"
'Psychic Psychedelic'
'Streaming Lemon Topaz Sunbeams'
'Invasion of Beauty *FLASH* The Love Mudras'
'Patchouli Showers ~ Tantric Temples'
'It's Just a Story ~ We Are All The Sun, Sweet Surrender'
Anthology #1 ~ 'Enjoy The Revolution'
Anthology # 2 ~ 'Love & Freedom ~ Welcome'
'He Lives In a Parallel Universe'
'Queen of Space ~ King of Flower Power ~ dripping Rainbows'
'All Love Frequency ~ In Zero Space'
*Peace Goddess*Spirit of the Field*The Intimacy Sutras*
'Heavenly Bodies ~ Celestial Alignments
Feeling ~ Energy that Is LOVE in Itself'
'I've been to Venus & back*These Are Real Feelings*
Let the Universe Guide Your Heart*through Space'
The Kiss in Slaughterhouse 6

'During times of universal deceit, telling the truth is revolutionary'. Orwell
'In 2017 there are **five** men who collectively own as much wealth as the
poorest half of the global population, new research from Forbes shows.
As Oxfam before, it warns that the gap between the super-rich and the
very poor keeps on widening every year. In 2016, it was the world's 62
richest people whose combined wealth equated that of the poorest 3.6
billion on the planet. 'The net worth of the Rothschild family has been
estimated at anywhere between $US 1 trillion and $US100 trillion. They
are thought to control the Bank of England, the European Central Bank,
the Federal Reserve, the World Bank, International Monetary Fund and
Bank of International Settlements. They own most of the world's gold
and the London Gold Exchange'. They and their cronies apparently own
the rest of the World's wealth. (The Paradise Papers on Tax havens).
These Plutocracies exploit the world's resources to acquire everything.
Their wealth dictates society, politics, economics, wars we all live under.
The state of Planet Earth today is a direct reaction to their fascist greed.
Capitalism, debt, poverty, GMO/natural destruction, extreme inequality,
derive from their mismanagement, to keep us divided and conquered ~
so maintaining their continuous positions, of unholy, sociopathic Power

Mysticism

*Mysticism from the Greek ~ (muo, 'concealed')
is the pursuit of achieving communion or identity with, or
conscious awareness of, ultimate reality, the divine, spiritual
truth, or God through direct experience, intuition, or insight;
and the belief that such experience is an important source of
knowledge or understanding. It may involve a belief in the existence
of realities beyond immediate perceptual apprehension, or a belief
that true perception of the world goes beyond intellectual apprehension,
or that 'beingness' is central to all perception.*

*

*Mystics generally hold that there is a deeper, more fundamental state
of existence hidden beneath the appearances of the day to day living
(which may become, to the mystic, superficial or epiphenomenal).
For the mystic, the hidden state is the focus, and may be perceived
in any of various ways - as God, ultimate reality, a universal presence,
force or principle, psychological emancipation ~ and be experienced or
realised directly. Such experience are spoken of variously, as ecstatic
revelation, theosis, direct experience of the divine or of universal
principles, nirvana, enlightenment, satori, samadhi, etc*

*

*They are sometimes characterised by a fading or loss of self,
or a perceived interconnection with all existence, and are
often accompanied by feelings of peace, joy or bliss.
Mysticism is usually understood in a religious context,
but as William James (1902) points out, mystical experiences may
happen to anyone, regardless of religious training or inclinations.
Such experiences can occur unbidden and without preparation at any
time, and might not be understood as religious experiences at all.
They may be interpreted, as artistic, scientific, or other forms of
inspiration, or even dismissed as psychological disturbances.*

With that in mind, the word 'mysticism' is best used to point to conscious and systematic attempts to gain mystical experiences through studies and practice. Techniques include meditation, prayer, asceticism, devotions, the chanting of mantras or holy names, or even intellectual investigation. While mystics are generally members of some religious denomination, they typically go beyond specific religious perspectives or dogmas in their teachings, espousing an inclusive and universal perspective that rises above sectarian differences.

*

James points out that a mystical experience displays the world through a different lens than is present in ordinary experience. The experience, in his words, is "ineffable" and "noetic"; placed beyond descriptive abilities of language. While there is debate over what this implies ~ whether, in fact, the experience actually transcends the phenomenal or material world of ordinary perception, or rather transcends the capacities of perception to bring the phenomenal and material world into full view. Mystics focus on the experience itself, and are rarely concerned with ontological discussions'. ~ from Wikipedia, the free encyclopaedia.

*

<u>Six Sided Pointed Star</u>
Gold put inside my heart
from the Angels ~ Alchemy of the Cosmos
Coming through Mother Earth, Unrealised, surely they
Realise the mess that exists, that they're getting rich off!
Who wants plastic when there is hemp? Used for everything!
Who wants a plastic brain, who wants a field of hemp?
Who left a couple of bombs, destroying a Varanasi train?
Allowing Spirits to Unfold in exploding particles on the Ghats!
In essence ~ In*Spiralisation being in the Present moment.
Nothing more to do but be and see and feel freely allowing
rivers of grace to take you floating endlessly ~
"Too much going on Inside my Mind"

Related graffiti of a 'legal' gang, called 'Dina'
Absolutely No Rules and Regulations darling ~
"The grass, might be greener on the other side but
it's just as hard to cut." It's the one that gets water.
"My mother made me a lesbian", she confided to me.
"If I give her the wool will she make me one too?"
What choice: You shoot me, or I shoot you, dead first!
Choice of? Democratic Parliament; Spineless Politicos!
He changed the Law, to suit himself; not those he tortured.
Supported by the Army of course; let Pinochet go free? WTF!
Swords piercing your body, just stay with the Sensations.
Lots of Predators circling, full cruel treatment by Demons.
"You're allowed a 'Non-human', with an electrified vagina!"
Hung him from the walls, practiced karate on his spine.
*
Atomic Bomb of Love
"Don't do that Sunny, what will people Think!"
"Earth is the Heart Chakra of this Nazara Universe"
They left bombs in Japanese playgrounds,
I left my body for some light in the dark…
left shells from Plutonium in Iraqi nurseries.
Everything's a big banging, expanding milky way!
Arriving on the island in violet flames, channeling ~
Jimmy Hendrix, Elvis, Marilyn, Hermes and hippie
friends ~ Life is sweet jumping into a pool of Love.
In Lands of the psychedelic, opalescent, peace dove.
*"Jesus' Spaceship * 'Nesarath' landed in an olive grove.*
Transmutation ~ Changing with the right frequency…
Now the Mirrors are getting stronger into Beingness."
*Indigo children allowed * to unfold sublime moments.*
Dissolved a gorgeous, hybrid clone.
Living the Ideal, 'in it not of it ~
"Oh, God what a beauty!"

San Francisco Chronicle, Monday, August 7th 2006
Half of US believes Hussein had WMD.
by C. J Hanley, Associated Press.
Poll finds myth endures despite debunking;
many blame talk radio, blogs, White House.
"Do you believe in Iraqi WMD?" Did Sadam Hussein's
government have weapons of mass destruction in 2003?
Half of America apparently still thinks so, a new poll finds, and
experts see many reasons why: a drumbeat of voices from talk
radio to die-hard bloggers to the Oval Office, a surprise headline
here or there, a rallying around a partisan flag, and a growing
need for people, in their own minds, to justify the war in Iraq.
People tend to become "independent of reality" in these
circumstances, says opinion analyst Steven Kull.
The reality in this case is that after a 16 month, $900-million plus
investigation, the U.S. weapons hunters, known as the Iraq Survey
Group, declared that Iraq had dismantled its chemical, biological
and nuclear arms programs in 1991 under U.N. oversight.
That finding in 2004 reaffirmed the work of U.N. inspectors,
who in 2002/03 found no trace of banned arsenals in Iraq.

*

Despite this a Harris Poll released July 21 found that a full 50% of
US. respondents up from 36% last year, said they believe Iraq did
have the forbidden arms when U.S troops invaded in March 2003,
an attack whose stated purpose was elimination of supposed WMD.
Other polls have found an enduring American faith in the WMD story.
Timing may explain some of the poll result. Two Republican Law -
makers, Pennsylvania's Sen. Rick Santorum and Michigan's Rep. Peter
Hoekstra, released an intelligence report saying 500 chemical munitions
had been collected in Iraq since the 2003 Invasion.

"I think the Harris Poll was measuring people's surprise at hearing this after being told for so long there were no WMD. in the country" said Hoekstra spokesman Jamal Ware. But the Pentagon and outside experts stressed that these abandoned shells were 15 years old or more, their chemical contents were degraded, and they were unusable as artillery ordnance. Since the 1990s, such "orphan" munitions, from among 160,000 made by Iraq and destroyed, have turned up on old battlefields and elsewhere in Iraq, ex-inspectors say. In other words, this is no surprise. "These are not stockpiles of weapons of mass destruction." said Scott Ritter, ex-Marine who was a U.N. inspector in the 1990s. "They weren't deliberately withheld from inspectors by the Iraqis" Conservative commentator D. Murdock, who trumpeted Hoeksta's announcement in his syndicated column, complained in an interview that the press "didn't give the story the play it deserved" but in some quarters it was headlined. "Our top story tonight, the nation abuzz today" Was how Fox news led its report on the old, stray shells. Talk-radio hosts and their callers seized on it. Feedback to blogs grew intense. Kull and others see an influence of opinion that's more sustained than the odd headline. "The basic dynamic is in the insistent repetition by the Bush administration of the original argument" said John Prados, author of the 2004 book, "Hoodwinked: The documents that Reveal how Bush Sold Us a War." Administration statements still describe Hussein's Iraq as a threat. Despite the official findings, Secretary of State, Condoleezza Rice has allowed only that "perhaps", WMD. weren't in Iraq. And Bush himself, since 2003, has repeatedly insisted on one plainly false point: that Hussein rebuffed the U.N. inspectors in 2002. The facts are that Iraq, after a four year hiatus in cooperating with inspections ~ acceded to the U.N. Security Council's demand and allowed experts ~

to conduct more than 700 inspections of potential weapons sites from November 27, 2002 to March 16, 2003. The inspectors said they could wrap up their work within months.
Instead, a US. invasion aborted that work.

*

"Naturally, the common people don't want war, but after all, it is the leaders of the country who determine the policy, and it is always a simple matter to drag people along, whether it is democracy, or a fascist dictatorship, or a parliament, or a communist dictatorship. Voice or no voice, the people can always be brought to the biddings of the leaders. It is easy. All you have to do is tell them they are being attacked, and denounce the pacifist for lack of patriotism and exposing the country to danger. It works the same in every country".
Hermann Goring, Hitler's Reich-Marshall
at the Nuremberg Trials, after WW11

*

"Beware the leader who bangs the drums of war in order to whip the citizenry into a patriotic fervour, for patriotism is indeed a double-edged sword. It both emboldens the blood, just as it narrows the mind. And when the drums of war have reached a fever pitch and the blood boils with hate and the mind has closed, the leader will have no need in seizing the rights of the citizenry. Rather, the citizenry, infused with fear and blinded by patriotism, will offer up all of their rights unto the leader and gladly so. How do I know? For this is what I have done.
And I am Caesar." (Julius Caesar)

*

"Don't the Bible say we must love everybody?"
"Oh the Bible! To be sure! It says a great many things. But then, nobody ever thinks of doing them".
From, 'Uncle Tom's Cabin' by Harriet Beecher Stowe.

Paramo of bedazzled Grasshoppers
Who is that Universal Monarch ~
with the brightest colours on his wings?
We're on holiday, not bearing our hearts.
So let's take it up, 'Pre Programmed' Performer.
Giving you a bit of a buzz ~ Chi, a Free Spirit.
Never been easy to shut the blinging Mind.
My energy is on the rise, its just given in,
connecting to the People ~ Vibration
*

Bhagwan's Vespa
"Oh So beautiful ~"
through swami's lovely eyes.
Bring it on up ~ Time flies.
Sincere ~ to touch the Stars.
"I'm not suitable to live with another person"
I Love the beach.
*

Gina Lollobrigida's smiling eyes
"that's the sort of thing that happens to me! Unbelievably,
Sig. Bellini and Fellini driving a Bugatti in Pondicherry!"
Have some of that! What comes after the dreaming?
I always wanted to meet Venus with fluore Red hair.
A Mad Scientist fell in Love with her; sparkling
Paramour. "I don't know if I can stand up!"
Empty the Mind, clear and Open.
Bottom line? Is to be ~ Free
*

'I'm now Officially, literally Your Ex!'
I want to meet 'My Self's, 'Own' Ex!
We all live in a fascinating Pantomime.
Accepting other people's Rights to be stupid…
With a raging Sikh, in a 'War of Onions and potatoes'.
The price went up by 3 Rupees!

The Hiding Brain ~ Psychic Boundaries
Squatting for a bit of Freedom, taking a Mortgage holiday!
'Keep on smiling the whole World will smile with you.'
"You promised" ~ "Well I'm taking my promise back!"
"Stand up for your rights." "As God is my witness!"
"Don't lose Your Prayer" Society - A System! Free Spirit ~
Not Institutionalised; a Psychedelic, Punk from San Marino.
"Who didn't paint a Church somewhere around Florence?"
'She worked in an Italian Restaurant in Newcastle on Tyne'

*

Trusting * Healing
Try to be an Angel to someone.
You feeling the Love in your heart ~
And Luciferians of Deception, selfish, heartless Love!
Love bulbs glowing in her seductive, Quauntum heart.
Runs on frequencies, those going off together in bliss.
We'll soothe, detox it with our higher consciousness.
Vibrating her ever so sweetly.

*

Meditation Path
Concept of the future, 'People over Profits'
which doesn't exist. What's the direction?
Only focusing on the clear Space of now ~
Chemical reaction * fractal bouquets of Lotuses.
'It's better to have had it than not to have had it'
The energy of creativity goes there to expand!
Pink Pages cliches, Ads from the 50s. 'Speaking for Itself'
"Smoke these and you can look like Audrey Hepburn!"
Demand & Supply, Supply & Demand, Supply & Demand.
The Vatican Never condemned the Nazi Genocide! Bang!
1000 deserters from the British army in Iraq in three years!
Authorities refusing to accept it has to do with the Invasion.
New mantra ~ No one wants War

Plus Prudent

You can fuck people's Minds just with negative words!
Buddha's or any Religion; word God is only just a word.
Only Man-Made atoms, Anger is human. Your very own,
misconception, misdirection, misperception, misalignment.
Tribals coming from Instinctive juice, are being dictated to.
Perversion is some form of Suppression of Creativity ~
too many Rules, Regulations, moralists; Ego can't deal
with it, we become out of balance ~ whirling Ambience.
If You can't Love Yourself, can You Love Anyone else?

*

New Spectrum Drone

'US criticizes Israel for illegal use of their Cluster Bombs!'
Designed specifically to make their Bombs, explosives;
explode so very silently! You can sleep right through it.
Like a cosy mattress. "Hatred is the Shadow of Your Ego"
The Opposite of Love Is Fear ~ Integrity not more polarity.

*

Nectar * Contact

Psychiatrists don't really have a clue, can you believe it?
Right off the track, living it for real, not out of a textbook.
"Couldn't even Kill a fish ~ that eye's always open!"
Who has been holding the light then?
To have a House with No doors or windows, totality.
Others swore Acid was the fuel, the Magic door ~
No expectations, No Fear in Fearless Meditation.
'Eye to Eye not an Eye for an Eye ~ we all go blind'

*

Wisdom Is Wisdom

"I can agree with you"
Glad to hear it mate ~ so am I.
"Where are we going?"
"We're going to War!"

Selling '1984 Insurance': Threats > What to work on?
Tarts, "What are Your Dreams, what are Your Fears?"
"They gave us 'Individuality' ~ to Control us even easier"
Sent You to the Salt Mines, going over the edge of waves.
Menacing Again > remote committees of devoted drudge.
'Disappointed they didn't get to see the Public Hangings!'
Their ferocity turned outside, against the Demon Enemy.
Denounced them to the Party disciples, 'Thought Police'.
"We shall meet in the place where there is no darkness"
*

Whoever You Are in a World of Lies
Karma dancing on the Moon with your ecstatic Free Will
Singing bhajans with Agoris and dhobi wallahs at Benares.
No Propaganda, No brain-washing, No Fear Stalking me.
Covering my tracks, not hiding out of sight from the light.
'You've got the wrong number' ~ take Your Responsibility.
Ultimately Power is in your hands; Heart, Mind up to You!
'Thought Crime' couldn't conceal the guilt of it, the Paranoia.
These self confessed, self empowered, sole guardians of
Truth & Sanity. Their World of lies and spies that terrifies!
From in their locked loneliness of dark and fearful reality,
their rage, vindictive hate, torture, seems as an electric flow
of odious, regressive, rhythmic impacts on your 'I ball' ~
Don't accept the ulterior motives of a crashing Kamikaze.
They exist in their own, inconceivable imaginary Doomsdays.
For me, existing in the sparkling crystals of being ~
Self Conscious of my Power to change;
Power to live my life of freedom….
Your choice, to let them take you to an Unjustified War!
Don't blame the other sheep, wolves, sows or holy cows
If Life is what You want it to be from Inside your Heart.
Not their fault that you became enlightened
I chose to love you ~ Perfectly here now

Timeless ~
Have you ever heard of Dolphins fighting?
I'm a Unicorn in disguise ~
Communicating with Humans.
From an Infinite Source

*

No Questions
"Go and Make a chapatti!"
Being Useful ~
"You have to give shelter", It's in the code…
Living with Real Knowledge of the country.
Genuine Shivaette ~

*

Trishul Power
From telling the Truth, clearly.
At least You were honest ~
from a Real Invasion of You!
"You bring a rule in here and I'll kick your head in!"
"I'm against the whole idea of National Anthems"
Need to get rid of Inbred Parties and be Independents.
Stood up, "I did it for the struggle and respect of India."
How can anyone Justify landmines and the biggest slum in Asia?

*

These Places
Surreal kaleidoscopic, the Giraffe Pub in Kennington.
It never really existed ~ until You actually find them!
"Dr. Kelly from the Bahai, a Very Mysterious Martyr."
The Powers that Be, 'Their Law' can get away with it.
They are devising the rules, calling and making the shots.
"Accidents don't happen like that mate." No blood evidence.
Told by a professional; bring back the True Democracy.
"If in any doubt take the Happy Path, for Sure!"

Full Bright I*deal * Idealic
When you fall into somebody's eyes ~
Magical realism of great Goa Vibrations.
"I'm under No delusions why I take drugs!"

*

What an Act! See www.wmdthefilm.com
To sell War, to sell Conquering, Invasion, as Liberation!
Who is Selling all these Terror Weapons of Destruction?
What's their Spiel and Track Record on Holy Crusades?
What does it say on their Curriculum Vitaes?
What's it say in their Glossy Obituaries?
Always getting caught out in an Untruth.
"One Man's Lie is another Man's Sales Pitch!"
Found myself between Iraq and a hard place.
They're not Accounting for the Whole truth!

*

Any Violence Is Horrible!
"Gave him a 'Bamboo Massage' as a courtesy!"
"The first night she lived there someone jumped off the 1ˢᵗ floor!"
I left due to loss of Rights, Yob Culture, the Police State!

*

Cui Bono?
Redefining what it is to be human now? "I Love You"
No free Space being continually connected to the cloud?
That is your environmental domain; prison cell or natural?
Would you like some 5G. Intelligent wallpaper projections?
Living in a smart grid, not a living Planet called Mother Earth.
Omnipresent Internet, processing 100 billion micro-nano chips.
A Global, NWO. brain communication, centralising all our data.
Systems with cognitive intelligence ~ you are now a little Robot.
Transformational digital age; do you have an Android? Yes, I do.
Do you have a programmed-bot, 'Replika' or physical-biological?
Welcome to the latest Panopticon, monitoring system brother.
Cybernetic feedback loop is not a revolution ~ or the seasons.

<u>Visible Energy Fields</u>
Planetary Symphony of Crystal Spheres ~
Actually, "I believe that I was the main problem"
Fauna, flora, every tree, it's all vibrating naturally.
Make it accessible to your sense consciousness ~
We come in Peace, please believe us one more time!
Why are we created from a frequency? Scan your DNA.
You are invited now to become enlightened, do you understand,
without any thinking; with bio-logical, not dualist, karmic mind-sets.
Altering, boosting, saturating; something has happened to you, what?
I am resonating Heavenly bliss of perfect harmony ~ this will change.
What are you truly aware of? Symbiosis, sharing in the Cosmic Love.
You are a drop in the Ocean and the Whole Ocean

*

<u>Watching the Stars fall</u>
A Loveless Marriage, 'Liberation is not upset by happiness or distress'
Who is being tortured humanely, with Advanced Stress Techniques?
They don't have the Death penalty; that means something positive!
Please don't make me leave Paradise to witness public executions.
You have been Invited to visit Planet Peace, no conflicts there…
Are you afraid, full of fear and scary paranoia? I wonder why?
Brainwashed, pre-conditioned; I didn't know what I was seeing.
Out of balance, I, my mind's ego wandering all over the place ~
can't distinguish any life-form, do they have feelings; compute?
Each experience is a stepping stone, transforming for the best.
We have integral Power to choose, ascend or fight for Peace ~
Seeking Unity in diversity or superiority, tyranny, which is more
Real to you? To live in constant illusion or unconditional Love ~

*

He was an unconscious madman from the beginning.
The deeper feelings that make you think and wonder.
If you're not happy with her or him; it's within yourself ~
Let Life flow through the karmic conditioned Mind-drive.
Flowers that dance ~ reaching to the Heavens of free Love

Relax
be calm, my destiny is go to the Stars.
I don't want to become Possessive ~
"Can't make someone Love You."
Evaluation & Comparison…
"god you're gorgeous!"
*

'Mitra'
A Gautama with tears on his cheek!
'Calling the Troops, calling the Tribe'.
The beauty is Choosing us ~ let it flow.
*Full treasure * jewels of the divine Yoni Pearl.*
not Obsessional edges and More Fire Power!
"Everything we've done is Forgiven, everything.
We don't have to think like that anymore ~
We're together now"
*

Locked for Your Own Protection >:< Not If but when!
An Anti-Culture? Open Mind of Om but No Aumness ~
Propaganda of Negative, dark, lifeless, System Machines.
Self-hypnosis, fall in and copy it like everyone else, or else!
Expressions in his eyes might conceivably betray him, to Music,
associated with Pride, Patriotism, horror and guilt ~ what about
those who simply disappeared into the angry, Andean volcanoes?
Having been forgotten, no trial, no report of the arrest, no Existence.
There's no records that you ever lived on this planet as a real being!
You have been Wiped out, deleted all Memory, wiped clean, gone,
abolished, annihilated, obliterated, Vaporized, in front of our eyes!
Fearful, paranoia, terrified, waiting for a knock at our door for sure.
Heart's thumping, being erased; denying your true human nature.
Instinctive reactions, our overwhelming emotions my darling.
Out of Control, I do remember that we did Love each other.
Naturally, Freely, Truly, Openly, Ecstatically and Forever.
"If you're Happy, You have to go Up!" For sure ~

Can't Predict

Ultimately it's Communication, Hallo, Salut, Da.
Good, Bad, Indifferent, Size, Wise, Realised ~
That's the Apparent question, are you Aware of it,
Or Not? You know your destiny to be Consciousness.
Who are You really, that's 'Human conditioning'.
Breathe and Focus ~ Breathe and Focus.
No need to put Reiki or drops in my Chai!
People do get wrapped up; In Reactions ~
What's the matter with this? Nothing at all...
People being them themselves, don't get sucked in...
It's there for a reason ~ Realise true Awareness of Space,
She could stick up for herself, inside, knowing beyond mind!
"Who are You to say I can't laugh?"
*

Detours of the Tripping Mind

"He never ate meat after his conversation with a cow"
Can't wait for tomorrow, Fantastic ~ If you are not
actually doing it; it's the Mind drawing the pictures.
"Why Parties are Like Meditation; Pulls People In ~
The Love Vibe is going on ~ not any poisoned dream."
He belonged to the Society for the Protection of natural
MDMA. in a culture of Rackets! Getting into his Starship.
They resisted and revisited; pulled it right in ~ Whack!
It's the Truth, just embrace it, as soon as the other starts,
drop It, drop the limited Mind, can't beat the Divine in Bliss.
*

Wholesome Portal

"Too much going on, thoughts in my Mind!"
Conceived on a Total Om ~
The Poems of dream
Your face lights up
when you smile
Spreading it ~

<u>The doorway</u>

Lovely living on the riverbank ~
"Pythagoras, Look at that, that's a Cracker!"
Pilgrimage ~ Bombshells, on the streets of Devon.
Part of the Unavoidable, Order of things…
Their Lives Sacrificed for what? A cold War!
Swept the corrupt Authorities into Nothingness ~
The Underground, Undercover, Overt, Covert, Alert!
Very disappointed in their Purges, those Crazy Pogroms.
"It was not by being heard but by staying Sane
that the Human heritage was carried on"
"For Survival he recognised himself as a New Age Rebel"
The Sun light family, left for you to remember; a fertility
hope, to retrace the meaning of Your true Self 'Identity'.
Their dead eyes pursuing you everywhere, watching you.
Invading into you with feelings that there is 'No Escape'.
Totalitarianism, to Annihilate a Whole culture; all futility.
Wiping out all Traces, of their Crimes against Humanity!
*

<u>Real or Dream Worlds</u>

So many cameras, You can find Terrorists anywhere in UK!
Nakedly ~ getting rid of whole Systems of thought.
Who told you? "You're the Poet with blue eyes" ~
'We always Want, what we don't have' & Vice Versa.
What do you feel like? Greeting a Walmart breeder…
How long do you expect me to watch you Torture, Poison,
slowly destroy Yourself; ignorantly, Unconsciously, darling?
A 4XAlpha Vikingbot, Insanely shooting up to the stars!
"Full tripping, driving his bike to outer Space ~ Inside."
Still Raging, "Now you wake up!" You Flipped…
to be a part of that feeling! Everything's on Sale.
Super Pixies or part of the 'Big & Better Deal'
Sacrifice not Compromise, she got her wish,
female Instincts! Speed dating, infatuation.

Totally Unacceptable
Sounds crazy; no she was just being her Self. "I was Crazy!"
'Putting their cross in that box' and getting it hacked for free.
There's always an effect unless you became enlightened.
Awareness of No Violence, No Violence! Does it help?
"What You Expose them to; expose them to dirt,
they'll live in dirt!" "I wanna be ~ drama free"
*

5G Omnipresence
Whatever happened to being Conscious of the here and now?
Never again being disconnected from the Global brain of God.
Nano-sensoring your bio-data, ask your local mobile provider.
Caught in the web of a dangerous spider with cognitive dissonance.
Analyse and records everything, opening the black box of your cortex.
What happened to a Free society, Freedom of thought; always a Myth!
Always been slavery, coffles, now it's controlled by insensitive Robots.
Do what your told or you will be punished, even for having a thought.
"People need to put down their phones and wake up"
Looking into black mirrors, mind being hypnotised.
*

Dividing and Conquering Us
Sociopathology, All means justify the End; to them!
Doing what they're told, "Get the Mission done!"
To be a Predatory Super, World Power, Empire.
To be at the Top table ~ bring the list…
Who has read, The Wolfowitz Doctrine?
This is what to do to achieve your result!
1 World Order > How do you do it ~ the Catalyst?
Pick from the Menu, Ideological silo. You want ~
A Government take-over, brutal, economic sanctions…
Anonymous Assassination, Military coups, Terrorist attacks,
Secret Army mutinies, Dictators specially made to Order?
The Deep state carving their cruel Totem of blood and gold!
*Another Stray Missile! Into the dark * into the Light.*

Lollipops of the Guru chick!
"They'll do Cocaine till the cows come home."
'The Patriot Actors', wrestling, Big Macs, Jesus & Nascar!
"Another Perfect Sunday; see you in the Office Monday"
*

Jackass
"Smoke and he didn't Inhale or penetrate!"
'Don't Ask Don't Tell' Policy'. What bullshit...
They Know; I thought it was a Myth, just bad PR!
Don't Push too hard, If you give him less to live for ~
becomes a Dangerous Ding Dong
*

mICROsOCIETY
A 'Blanket Party!' You know what I mean?
Everyone gets a Hit, Informal Codes, duties.
'Life's all about People's Lives you wouldn't believe'.
Got a Dear John Letter, from his girl ~ Jumping Ship!
Only 5% of US, have Passports, Memberships of...
'A bunch of Forest Gumps'. 'Fortunate Son of mine'
"If a guy can't throw a Punch but he can kick you
and you can't see it, You're gonna get Kicked!"
"Smoke Him Out!" - Frat boy who wants to be a Cowboy.
The Charisma, Oil Is Oil, black gold; All in Oil a Sales Job!
What tomorrow brings, another Chimpanzee or Democrat?
"The Chinese bought a lot of US. shit!" They Own You...
'Money Is Money' ~ as long as it all comes back as $$$.
Free Expressions, the Ego Trickles Down, Capital Effects!
And 1% of the Population is in Prison, highest in the World!
There's a baby born in Jail every six hours; Land of the Free!
Who's Pushing those Insane Buttons? "Pushing it Yourself!"
He's All for evolving through the Soft Machine ~
"Cryogenicise my DNA. and shoot me to Venus"
What Works, what doesn't Work; In Science!
"When It Goes It Goes"

The Genie's Out the Bottle
'Fortress America' - Game of Winners & Losers.
We'll always Compete! # No Emotions ~
"How can we Best deal with the Realities?"
A Backhand job, getting around it!
The Idea Guy, "We'll make it Cool" but change nothing…
Who's Respecting Democracy? Others don't give a damn.
"Their extreme way, No delusions of Utopia." Profit baseline!
"How to Contain them and suck All the Energy out. Drain Dry!
Can be as Mad as you like at a Rich, Saudi Executioner,
not when you're driving to Ralphs for $2 not $6 a gallon.
Playing the Game, 'Balance of Power' by Oliver North!
"This is what we're really gonna do!"
*

HoodWinked
High Stakes Poker, such a distracting Fiasco.
We Want It Real! Thanks for visiting Alabama.
"You always Piss people off on the rise to the Top"
So We're just gonna 'Steam Roll' them!
His Terrortory and Glory! 'Operative of what?'
Good P.R. Keep them happy, Yeah, You dude!
"They're not goin' let him get his nose under the tent!"
When every one's working on themselves, can't be Conflict.
All working to better Ourselves! Better Entertainment…
Religion is Specifically designed Against this too.
It's all about Working for 'The Church's Ideology'.
In US. making yourself better means materially more comfortable,
a better situation, improving your leisure! Keep those hippies down!
The National guard. We helped the Indians, gave them TB, Blankets,
otherwise they'd still be sitting in their Tepees! Right Congressman?
Consciousness Streams ~ flowing. What happened to the Bison?
'It's not what Earth can do for You but what you can do for Earth'.
"Not that you want to do it but if you had to you could"
Bombing 'em with clusters of Loving Kindness!

Sweet test
Pink Petals of Love ~ make a wish!
It's happening ~ Life changes. "It's All Connected"
It's human, no ego, intention asking miracles to come true.
Don't be debt-enslaved mind, thoughts of Life without a name
or magic. Projecting what comes true for you ~ and me.
We're effecting Cosmically, giving and receiving naturally.
*

Birds of Paradise Mortuary
Take your share of the Responsibility for the Canopy.
We're the Stupid ones ~ we can't break their Code!
Spinning Dolphins and others massacred in Taiji Bay!
See the clouds passing by, the Planet's spinning ~
on its axis throughout the Galaxy of you inner-self.
When you gonna propose to your Pleidian girlfriend?
*

Captain of your Own Ship
Reached the High water mark of Pimpness!
"Let's go!" Totally taking the Piss!
'Il Principe', I hope I'm Not that smart, Ego.
"Snorting Railburners in the back country, BC!"
One day gonna have to let it go, sooner the better.
Always one F… little Mosquito! In Paradise ~
Paralysed, learnt to flow as drifting, crystal snow flakes.
From her Temple ~ jet streaming Indigo, It's on again!
Always ripping them off for their Light and Titicaca Water.
A nice Slam dude; You're either with them or against them!
You have to Understand, there's a lot of serious hatred ~
Frustration, with a Box Cutter and a fanatic, Iron Will!
"Stalin had more men than Hitler had bullets!"
Exploring the stars now, finding some mirrors.
Massage not Massacre, the Vibe of the Tribe.
"I wouldn't like us either" ~ for Real!
*Being in a Perfect * Invisible Circle*

With Him Eye to Eye Within

What is your Exposure, Alignment, fractral holography?
"1200 mikes of Acid says that you're Clinically Insane!
They're very afraid and very suspicious of it", my friend.
Unlocking the vaults big time, of Cosmic Perceptions.
"The Zeeboys. Skateboarders from Dogtown, half flipped.
Took their Culture and gave them MS118 & 24/7 Bingo"
'Here's the funny farm of the World ~ that's the Mission.
To Open People's Mind-paradigm as the boundless Universe.
Taking Individual responsibility in context with everyone else.
"Sometimes I wonder why I talk"

*

Undrownable, no shit!

Just seen the revolution in Shinzin with the fungal bros.
Mata India, Close Knit, 54% of Pop. below 25 years old!
Are you on their Mailing Lists, sent it to the Wrong Gaff.
Changing with a Plan, from Opium fields to Strawberries.
"On every Street corner in New York ~ dude,
there's a Nigerian with a briefcase!"
Don't get caught, hooked into ABCDE, Blah blah bla.
Seeing into and virtually through, 'A Scanner Darkly'.
Borrowing from the Chinese makes America Greater!
Surveillance * a camera for every 14 people in the UK!
Creating a Robot Police State >!< Jamming Underground.
'Step Forward, Welcome to Monty Python in brown shirts.
'Lost in Translation Again, "I'll put my life on the Line for
You and Your son will put his life on the Line for me!"
Did you get your 40 acres and a mule yet brother?
Holocaust > Reparations ~ for Everything on Earth.

*

The Soft Machine Motto

"Any man doing a Job is working to make himself Obsolete."
"Language is a Virus" from outer Space * New Prototypes!
Spinning and Spiraling ~ W. S. Burroughs

Governing
And "The Gulf War Syndrome don't Exist mate"
Blame the People who caught it ~ Don't Panic!
The CIA. will implant, straight into your vein, to your brain.
Providing blacked out goggles in an Infinity swimming pool.
To pass the Test you only have to drown three times, for real!
All part of the Process, the ubiquitous Matrix.
"How many folks are working on that Shift,
with their fingers on which nuclear buttons?
And Jesus Freaks? ~ All Parts, cogs of the Machine."
Old Timer don't Underestimate the Power of Your Love,
the depth of your own beautiful Illusions, the strength of
the Image of your desire. The almighty Pain of your Loss ~
She Lives nearby with someone else, taking it Very seriously!
"You can't Make them Love You or even listen to you, can you?"
In the psychic meadows of breaking hearts.
Lesson No. 1, as a Rule of Thumb.
Keep facing the Truth and Smile ~
At The Apocalypse
*

Slaves on Waves
Le Joie de Vie, trying to be true to Life ~
She was free, a new Goddess from Venus.
It's illegal to have Parmesan in the fridge!
"You're allowed to be fat when you are rich!"
People were going to school with a syringe!
"Such a horrible feeling when you stand on a snail"
"You don't find Russians who are gluten intolerant!"
"It's a good deal when everyone walks away Happy!"
What we want is justice for every being in the world.
The Earth breathes life through the oxygen of its trees!

<u>Durga's Summer Rain</u>
"Life Is Good ~ You can Choose, Your Free will."
"If in doubt ~ Choose the Happy Path for sure!"
Mania, OCD. let it go ~ an Invisible Mosquito.
Natural synchronicity, "I'm saving the trees."
Cell with a view, when You dance for Freedom.
What's after the Party, Party, Free Party.

*

<u>She's Enhanced Wacko</u>
Dedicated Interrogator...
Everything is False on her. Created a new definition.
Legalised, US' 'Stress Techniques', a diabolic one!
Not considered by them to be; 'Inhumane Torture'.
Brains in their fat arses, sacrificial and sex slaves; Satanic.
Burning with Hatred, why bring Trouble? Blow up weddings!
Another Vicious Cycle has started ~ We're all blind now...
Is it worth spilling blood over? Married to his possessions.
No accidents in the Universe. It takes two to compromise.
They can land on the Moon but can't Stop making Wars.
No beginning, No End to Evil. Protection of the Dhamma

*

<u>Heart Light</u>
Go, Time is Ticking ~ Life Creations.
Stars, Aurora Borealis, dub on the beach,
clear Vision is good in the Middle, no extremes.
Love in Harmony ~ language is being Corrupted,
Uncorrupted, brain being hacked. More Pure Love.
Harmony Is Love ~ Stopping Mental programming,
limited Mind-sets, harmony eyes, bigger, expansive.
Lost in the Translation of it ~ It's Not that Important!
'Product' of your own thoughts, swimming in chaos.
Many want to be here now, witnessing only silence.
Inside, India Time, Slow down ~ be still, Understand
to enjoy Life as we are.

Oxymoron @ King Queen

Non-taxed offshore! "I won't go to war based on lies!"
'Control Dramas' Instinctively ~ You learn them.
They put out some vibe to get energy coming back.
'Insecurity'- Seeing through that, you don't Feed It,
so they don't get what they want, rentering the Matrix.
Demanding Attention, getting the Vibe ~ to have energy
flow back to what they want! The nipple, womb obsession.
Something else they get Addicted too, so hard to change it!
Are we so Invisible, can't see the truth, Madame Chameleon?
Maintaining the survival instincts, If animals cry, they're dead!
State sponsored Terrorism, don't make a mess with the Anthrax!
It's all a Mind-game; No feelings after 300 Crashes ~ detached.
With Love, Compassion, no more fear of that.
Angels on Earth in front of You, Inside of You.

*

Blacon Bindi Baba

Everybody's Worst Fear, a bad Prom date...
or Cluster bombs dropped onto others, mate!
No Sensitivity to the Suffering ~ what a state!
A Blast from the Past, Comrade Heart Kismet.
Working in the Plantation of small, slave faces.
"Let me call my wife, she knows everything!"
Master; Modernity Celebrity, mad Mythology of Caste.
Other People's Dramas! Coronation Street, going back
to the Village. You're the Most shocking person out, be ~
cause of the energy, most Unbalanced on the whole planet.
Slitting each other's throats, vicious murderous psychopath.
Not being ~ a Buddhist! Or the world would be inner Peace.
Romans and those, sweating like a rapist. Thumbs down!
Should sit you on a socket! New dawning, renunciation,
like a divorce, from a Guru or a demented spouse! ~Time
to change ~ can give you a new freedom to be Complete.
I left to tell the story

Green Is STOP ^ Red Is GO

Business > supply & demand ~ who's sharing energies?
Profits or Opportunities ~ Cheapest, best for Extraction!
Evolving with a pocketful of tricks to become a demon.
How many starved to death in Eden's wild meadows?
"Because I'm Really worth what to you?" Ask God.
L'Oreal; their Slogans Never miss a beat!
So Centred, a lovely gal on a Full Shiva.
So Centred, a lovely guy on a whole Vulva.
Natural, hard core, very chilled out ~ streams
*

Kudos for Her

Yo, baby give them some Millions ~ Not a Rap Concert!
Finland makes the World's Best sugar; au revoir Haiti!
Paradoxical, American Indian Casinos, richest Corporations,
being Controlled, stirring jealousies, keeping the tribe down.
'1st Nation Peoples' "I need You" Not dependent on the State!
Apparently you don't understand I had a scooter accident.
I was the Moon driving on the wrong side of the line ~
A big tidal Rip in Society, not Centred with Your Self.
'You shut your mouth and look at the pavement Chief'
"Massive Violence, Aggression; a death wish from Rio.
Will I be self-conscious, walk until you're under the Fort.
They're acting like a bunch of coke freaks Governor!
Mutation, evaluation, too edgy, please don't get mad.
Dao Indices, MDMA. LSD. meditation, looking centred,
in the mirror. Trance freeing your Mind from delusions.
Renunciation, so cool here; "I'm Not a Slave anymore."
Leaving someone You Love just to accept the way it is.
Took their Karma and said it was ok; destined to evolve.
Sensitive kind of person to energies ~ stay with the truth.
* Transcendental *
Freedom could be
Jesus in a Lotus

Head of a Wooden Horse
DMT. LSD. Enlightenment ~ Who is to say what is true,
what is entertainment, entanglement or Illumination?
Is it Window panes opening on ~ to the Universe?
OM is the essential ~ Vibration in everything
Riding the sparkling face of its crashing wave ~
it's what binds everything together, keep changing its Mantra Ray.
Migratory birds dance across the World's frequencies, Meditation
is just Conscious ~ 'Chill Out'

*

The Flock
'Recreational' escaping that Gravity
'Kundalini candy' ~ flying your way.
Caught with 44 papers * from Orion's belt!
"I was spreading Love"

*

Spartacus' Sparks
The American Model
"Shop Free Or Die"
"In the Mall right now!
Wandering and buying shit…
You can Fake anything under the Sun!
Best for his sake that he doesn't wake up.
Wondering ~ what did I do all those years?"
Stop to Shop

*

Glistening mouth
being at the same beach shack as the most beautiful,
sexually, chilled-out women in the World ~ every day!
Wonderful, golden, smooth skin of a super fantasia.
Intuitive feelings of heavenly bliss
drowning in your Moscow kiss ~
on the very verge of Paradise

Transcendence Is No Path
Through the houses of Scorpio and Neptune ~
Detachment is what happens, Karma candy his LSD.
glimpse beyond the Honey; a window open to the nectar.
When we're Identifying with what we're not, 'false Ego'.
"If we raise our Vibration ~ we'll see the Truth"
Changes the system; Powers of the Shanti Army!
*

Eyes down for 1200 mikes
Clearing the throat charka ~ just words, spells.
Absolutely, just looking and looking into forever.
They're f......g criminals, raping someone; predators not bridegrooms!
That's why we have natural laws; if angry get it off your chest; no fear.
The judge is working for the Crown. "Do you understand the charges?"
Government is the Trustee of my estate, I am its Executor, Beneficiary.
What's your number? Here's my Affidavit and a bill for any harassment.
I am not a Joinder, so I'm refusing to answer any questions.
Back to the Natural Law of the People, not Maritime Law.
"I move to dismiss this case." How about the supernatural?
Reincarnation ~ An I for an I, for another Pie in the sky.
Dalai Lama ~ arriving as Higher Conscious, Altruism.
Bottom line ~ what is the true Intention? Leading us to ~
Encroachment, fragmentation, Coke Cola, Empire's take -
over of Ubiquitos Space! Focus on his borderline genius.
Should be in an Institution; hey man, I'm free, travelling.
Man made Constructs ~ the Endless, 'War on drugs'.
"The Bigger the lie, the more people Believe it." Right!
Another War of Propaganda, who's pulling my strings?
Not Freedom of Speech, Use Your Common Senses.
Transgenders, testing their Social Consciousnesses ~
'If We raise the Vibration, we'll Live the Truth'
"Fuck you, You don't Know…
On a Love Jihad NOT Psychic warfare!"

Capsule Expansion

*The spaceships collided * Baltic Star Wars out there.*
A beautiful, svelte, Swedish module goes into Orbit ~
*Whatever's after outer Space * Inner Space * eternity*
*

Pusher Street

Who's read the Paradise Papers? As soon as you cop an attitude…
they got better ways to extort; another horrible virus, eugenic vaccine!
You got to know the Limit] searching for some sensation at the nose.
Checking his socks, laughing all the way home on the train.
*Tai Chi * Violet light, Cosmic Knight, Angels' Earth delight ~*
Shadows of the Planet on Fire, Inspiring intense desire.
"Fills me full of stoke, so much Coke to cut ~ spacey…
But on such a small surface, the best LSD on the planet"
Organic filters, tofu balls, mustard; I only work outdoors ~
spectrums of light, Heroin Lounge music, let that one go!
"Charlie with crazy, red neck cowboys, the Cocaine blues"
Colour of their slaves, shining, jet black panther eyes.
*

Good Trance Sending Cosmic Energy

*Lotus gardener * Environmental Protector ~*
Violets from a Red Sun, the Global Circus came to town.
"When I was travelling last year in Columbia…..
On tour with 'Venom', look at their reflections in the music."
A lovely, Brazilian, Japanese beauty, the one I left behind!
Don't Mind, don't Mind, I don't Mind, It's not a big deal, really.
When you're wrong, It's a good day when we can learn it.
In a Super Competitive Society, "One for All, All for Me"?
They want to buy this bullshit, "Do as I say, not do as I do!"
Don't get it from a book, don't get it on 42" HD. screen TVs.
Living in Shanti's smiles, gets it from Life ~ Transcendence
She's full Sufi ~ Living from the Heart.

Ecstasy Revolution
'As long as I make my own cider and grow my own weed'
Radiant ~ Yeah, some people are, enjoying la Dolche vita!
There's always value in saying, 'fuck it!'
'We all want a bit of cake; some people got all the cake!'
Everyone can have a miracle.

*

just free to be
*Programmed by another Smart Spirit * Messages to Earth…*
The Flowers of Life ~ Now it's full Celebration of a still Mind.
Open for that! A big Celebration for everybody, her Gallic spirit!
I'm not into Capitalism Investment or Neo-Economic Colonisation.
Different guises, surprises! ½ a drop anywhere, in a purring Vulvo.
Cosmic Star dust, essential molecules of Love ~ You and Your luck.
Clear reflections, Karma is multi-dimensionality holograms in Space.

*

Shaping ><>< Bioshifts
Free Spirit, this goes as far as you want ~ open your Imagination.
It seems to me < then you know it's all bullshit; good dimensions >
Opening the drum circle, Kosmic Poetic, Inspiration, tripping is ~
*Sacred Geometry * Perfect Symmetry * seeds of what?*
*'Freedom in the air' * as far as the eye can see.*
"And I'll believe it when I see it!"

*

Cosmic egg
Infinitesimal input ~ quantum cell in the electro-magnetic field.
Being kind to people why would you want to do anything else?
Coming from Source, how Inspired do You want to be?
What is the sense of this word, 'to know' that we use ~
Whatever we're living, it's the perfect Projection of Now.
Have you never been in love? Being deeper in the Heart.
*Sitting in Your chakra * Radiating from Source ~ naturally.*
The beaming, smiles of children, simply living it Innocently.

Uranium 1

Taking down the deep state, their slaves sold to paedophiles.
Unprocessed, every email, phone calls, from the last ten years.
Harvesting Lakota Indian children, selling them to venal Wall street.
Unbelievable, advanced Mind-control; welcome to the XXXXX files.
Mach 2, Sunburns, Zigzagging missiles, EMF warfare, NSA corruption.
Who lost $2 billion on the extra-terrestrials of Mars? Ask the Pentagon.
Free energy and water desalination, blooming in the lush, fertile Sahara.
Zionist trolls perfected digital assassination, disinformation, deformation.
Enemy agents of Global, Oligarchical paradigms on roads to damnation.

*

'Fourth Industrial Revolution'

Evolving humanity through the neo-delusions of High Tech.
Check the little perennial Robot in the pocket of your rocket.
Who's developed an Augmented Age, taking over all species?
Wandering dazed in our own I devices, in a web, of the internet.
Reinforcing the paradigm, brainwashing us. 'Yes, I do want a chip'
Falling in Love with your programmed chatbot; 'You are so real to me!'
Changing our natural sense, reality, for artificial worlds of digital things.
Redefining what it is to be human ~ Who is Free?

*

Welcome to the Pentagon Machine

DARPE- Defence Advanced Research Projects Agency.
Who is taking over from whom, what is their morality Caesar?
Being slaves to an I smart phone; telling you what life's all about.
Giving up your critical thinking faculty, never writing a Love poem.
Take them outside, shoot them by the wall, hang their heads on pikes.
The Kill decision is being made by unaccountable AI. machine drones.
We lost their algorithm functions, codes, a long time ago Mr. Dekard.
They have their own secret language, getting out of hand, the matrix!
We're their pets; repressed our human empathy for virtual apathy ~
Not everyone will get the same advancements, as per usual Lord.
24hr. surveillance; the wealthy elite are consolidating their Power!

The Sofa Man

"Matrix breeder sprawl fucked up all my Orange groves"
Energy Systems ~ getting more, more and more out of it!
His new Wife's name is SZHX1388 > Miss U. Topianasky.
Surfing at dawn in a socially engineered Myth. Barbarism.
It's not about God, it's what you believe in!
"The Dalai Lama, what's not to like about him?"
They're highjacking your Spirit

*

Jade Helm's Illusory, Sleight of Hand

"People got to stand up and grow their bollocks!"
They make Bombs, they'll drop Bombs; on You!!!
In the profitable business of fully murdering people.
Welcome to the Military Industrial Complex, USA et al.
SPIRIT OVER SOCIOPATHIC MIND OVER MATTER ~
Try this Psyche-active test. She's mad; an assessment.
Who has stolen the human race, their heart and soul?
Non-sensical threats; showing who really is in Control…
Troops on the street, feeling protected from any enemies.
Getting away with it; WTF made this scenario up and why?
Have you ever heard of SERCO? They're controlling your life.
"I can recognise a massive Ponzi scheme collapse when I see one."
"People living on the floor just because they stepped
on a land-mine when they were six!"

*

It's True Without a Word of a Lie

< Beam me In ^ Beam Me In! Man >< Mind >
Is it a Trap to deliver /\/\/ freely <:> Synchronicity ~
It's a matter of the channel, we are just transmitters
And receivers of that ^ frequency.::.>:.that|timing ~
*}}}}~~***~~^^^ just tuning into\ for Self-Realisations*
defined/\refined Acts of Nature* How can one begin
to figure that out/Why even 'Think' to figure that out?
'Love me like there's no tomorrow!'

31

Not Emotional War

Spiritual Sex * free tantric energy ~ Creative, Inspired again.
Always, "Spirit over Mind over Matter", as much as I realise ~
It don't matter, It's in the comin' down, it's in the goin' up; bein'.
Tripping through the Pathless Path ~ No Go Zoned, Patrolled.
The American sniper he met in Ecuador, stoned on speed and
Amphetamine; ½ the time thought they were on a video game!
We should all disarm ~ Counter Spinning. Carpet bombing is as
despicable as Nuclear bombing but Amazingly has become an
accepted Cabaret to these, collaterally damaged, reptile brains!
How? "When it's good it's good", otherwise it's a f…. nightmare!
"Acid felt very free to the bee enjoying the anti-authority honey."
Full on freedom bubbles and it's a lovely Vibe with good karma!
Got to go beyond that ~ is or it isn't, being in your human truth

*

Partying to Sensations

Metta, all square, now is it, "One for All and All for Me?"
Mitra, a friend, "No other Choice but to be Optimistic."
Looking towards Heaven, how many stars do you see?
Galaxies upon galaxies of Consciousness blossoming ~
Ten thousand petal Lotuses, blooming in the airstream.
Look Inside, feel how many more are opening…

*

Dunce's Hat

Name of a 'Gift of God' ~ this moment here.
Punishment of a Chief demon. Ganesh makes you happy.
When in Pain Land letting it flow ~ Om /so Simple, Sparkle.
I Love devotional people at the altar within, energy vibrating

*

ADA

All Dimensional Access///Our body will leave our energy ~
Prana, Life\Death/\Rebirth, "take it as a Pleasure, treasure."
Always journeying into Eternity, "If you Fear death, don't go ~
Controlling You, fear everything in this World!" Breathing in/~\out

<u>USA ~ Universal Spiritual Abundance</u>
All Aiming in the same direction/Cosmic infinities ~
One Heart //make your Own/relationship with the satGuru/
(no other Guru), Buddha, Yahweh, Jesus, Allah, the King, Divine
Emperor, the Holy Pope, the President, The Boss, the best Spouse.
Can't do it for You/:\holding a candle, alight in the middle of the night.

*

<u>One Giant Paradigm Shift</u>
'The Prince of Peace Snacks'// "burnt down Alexandria//
by a Bishop//Hallelujah////Co-creating; protect the coral ~
& hippocampus through Awareness, not greedy Ignorance.
God by any name, sister. Tremendous to be, Free Spirited.
No more Child Labour, Consumers you can make it happen!
characters::: Young girls too ready to Please You ~ Optical
Illusions, sleights of hand, Clear as a Bell; Electricity appears
'Permanent'. Real material as we are, and not on Atomic levels
of electronic light! Microns, 1 millionth part of a gram. 1200 Mics.
You'll get charged with Manslaughter; be seen as Clinically Insane.
Become Conscious, full respect, clear vision of a Shamanic healer.
Blasting out of gravity, galaxy of your Mind, floating Inner* Outer*
Infinite * Space, Perceptions & perspectives. How we see each ~
other. Uniquely, the drug is the drug ∧ gives the potency (fuel).
Whatever place you want to be and some you don't! Trust ~
A crocodile came into the kitchen, it's made of Crystal mirrors;
Ok! Wherever it wants to take you ~ coming down over Venus.
"I'm driving my scooter through the asteroid field", "Hallo Baba."
(Mind)* being Conscious ~ or an Addiction (Maya) to TV. Opium?
The Mind's Limits of Your Mind's thinking & the ability to swim It ~
So no overdosing, burn outs, flips, bad trips, mental come downs;
to free dive, to be Cosmically; she's wearing a dress of holograms.
A suit of Amour with beating heart and mind, dancing together
in Universal Space ~ Stars twinkling, high up in an infinite sky,
bright, golden trees of Autumn leaves swoon in glorious sunsets.
Journeying within my trip, out of mind, living deeply through Spirit.

*Our Spaceship * Pachamama*
Fuck the Wars, the Jihads, all this Terror-Ism's bullshit!
*"Let us Fight for Our Great Grandmother * Mother Earth"*
We're the Government, Media, we Love this monkey Mind.
Suspenseful measures, holding up the axe to nature, death!
I Know her ~
*

Getting the last bus home
Too much trouble sometimes, confused, running round ~ Inside out.
North pole, south pole, Levels of expectation, of Stress Vibrations.
It's true!
Maybe, You can't see it coming - a Policebot State!
The Surveillance, Programming, into your bedroom,
directly into your Inner sanctuary
*

Safe test drip
His whole family are serious alcoholics!
Never heard anything good said about that!
"Old people smoke Pot, don't want mushrooms or LSD.
Ordered them over the Internet! Username, Password..."
"They don't have a clue: 'Northern Lights', It's A B.C...
Powers given to the Drug Lord, Just have to Open Up!
Liberation ~ Depression, a depletion of happy Serotonin.
MDMA. Crashes through the Flood gates to Release it all!
Have to fly with that Trip ~ the way In and the way Out."
"I think", I don't need to Know Who I Am ~ all Illusory.
What do I Think anyway ~ what do I believe, I know?
Supporting Thinking, in the Full Material, Egoist West.
Free Mind ~ No more Attachments in the Spiritual East.
Observing yourself, Liberation of Spirit, the way Inside ~
Compassion context, concept; the Sun is Invisible Ecstasy.
The spectrum is alive, wave bands for you, me, Universally.

<u>"I Want It!"</u>
That same energy, inside * outside ~
The Spirit that moves through all things
Frequencies Advanced ~Just don't Stop!
The truth in her eyes * What you doin' it for?
You have to accept it or you torture yourself'
'Why give yourself Enhanced Stress Techniques?'
*

<u>I Believe In Parties</u>
She had INSATIABLE tattooed on her arse.
Have a party, pretty girls, bit of dancing.
No time for Jihad!
*

<u>Sexpot Castebot Dependent</u>
We are going to lose ourselves ~ totally recalling what base?
This is the dimensional frequency I was given to conform to.
Being human has always been about deciphering illusions!
Artificial, OBEY Cog. Intelligence, Consume dream program.
Identified by your electronic tattoo, this means you exist.
Can't enter the platform of critical thinking, where is life?
Where is Love, where is real weather, nature, humanity?
Entering Las Vegas, Disney World, with your brainwaves.
Editing our DNA code, autonomous software writing itself.
Making decisions over humans, virtuality becoming reality!
Vitality, what is real Maya? Different mind-sets of ignorance.
Where is spirituality, consciousness in all this Augmentation Lord?
*

<u>Real Raw Honey</u>
'Manali was the strongest, Kashmiri was the tastiest'
Blessed, blissed in the pool, swimming with snakes.
Make it clean, not vaccinations but basic sanitation!
Taking a pill getting rid of the pain but not its cause.
'They can't lock you up when you're free inside'
So why torture yourself?

Feeling Scared ~ Given Divine Protection
Breaking baby butterflies on the wheel of Iraq ~
And many, many more, corpses in flower gardens.
Annihilated the sweet, most intelligent in Rumi's orchards.
Killing, murdering their culture! Genocide is up before dawn.
Encroachment, fragmentation, Invasion, disintegration on impact!
Dividing and Conquering or "Love flow frees forever ~"
Blowing the Mind to bits, severing; Never so Clever!
Feel the Magic in the songs of Life giving Prana ~
"Only Love Will Get You Through The Night"
"Hanging from the fan ~ a bullet between the eyes"
*"Beam me in * beam me in"*
*

Beyond Sufi Love Cocoon
Still feeling Cosmic by Shiva's golden Moon,
still skipping the light fandangle's, new tune
still flying High ~ Psychedelia's Magic Lune
*still tripping, Imagination's * Surreal balloon.*
Look into the soul of my beating heart ~
touch the Spirit in my clear, bright eyes.
Inside the head of Chaos lies a surprise.
The whirling dervish ~ Vortex meditation.
Formless 100%, what do I Know?
*

Zone of My Spirit
"And he was such a nice kid" - "Welcome, to the Machine!"
"They had to sell their Souls to the Company, Robot Store"
Feeling Am I Mad, turning my back on a woman begging
with her child! Give me some balm, of that escapist kiss.
Give us all some mercy, from feeling Dhamma's bliss.
Some more Mystic Nirvana; Please help your self!
"We don't need any Forced Control" XXXXX factors.
All in All just another Cosmic Atom, inner Dimension.
A pulse vibrating, Inside my suit of amour

Beam me up. "We don't need no education or more conditioning!"
Carrying the Party with you. Mesmerized on their gross lies!
"I'm going on, right through it or I'll end up out of gas!"
Making it happen. Glad I snapped in ~ Cruising attitude.

*

Still morphed out
"His wife was a little hippie chick
in detox; he's perfectly normal,
goes to work, pays his taxes, married with kids.
To regular society she's a deviant! Can't admit it
but her brain's in the freezer, in Sacramento"
"A few customers and you're on top of the World!"

*

You could do it all!
'The Dr. Kevorkian of fruit juice'
"And every junkies like a setting sun!"
Law of viruses, told from the Chiefs' viewpoint.
That huge pandemic world is just there, microscopic…
Human Intelligence, Human Interpretation of everything.
I had that feeling at the back of my head, to trip into it ~
"Good to know someone in Estonia, Captain Xtrema
especially if they're in the Space Program!"
"The Estonian Spaceship has landed"
"The Spaceship's in the water" ~ She's on a Space trip
from the Estonian, Space Program, Central Command!
"Welcome back to Earth ~ you made it."

*

formless culture
Hallo, looking for absent friends, a thankless task you ask!
"With tender loving care, shaved all her fluffy, pubic hair."
A chiseled body and lips that felt like soft clouds to touch.
"She'll definitely need some strong Pepper spray in Mumbai,
to keep all them dudes away!" Sharing intimate secrets,
in coffee shops along Amsterdam's canals

Baby Pink Stars beyond Gravities of Mars
"There's someone in my head, but it's not me"
They made us think that it really, really matters...
Even though you feel ~ mystical sounds of silence.
You're on a spiritual path ~ glowing, spirals in her hair.
Hallucinations, Magic realism, haiku, super naturalness ~
thinking, Zen, decoding, Intellectual Associations, secrets,
conceptions, polarities, dualities, projections of extremities.
Ultra Yin * Yang, spiralling comets in the celestial firmament.
It's just consciousness being infinitely conscious ~
Illumination of your Mind not limitation * elimination.
Absolutely stormin' unpredictable, that's where it lives.
Horns in the head, Incandescent flames can cross over.
Infra-Landscapes of Relativity and Psychedelica Cosmica ~
Abstractions between your smiling, open wet lips, rosy cheeks,
caressing, gripping thighs, bio electro-magnetism, sparkling Love.
Meteors arise inside her eyes, sublimely, aimed through your heart.
Venus, she has perfect peaches ~ diamond stardust, twinkling auras
*

Generia ~ The Full Power Shake
It's All in the modern Mall, a nano-Homerbot.
If you don't want to be part of it - The Machine
don't complain, does what its programmed to do.
Found you in a Marriage chapel, soaking wet in the rain.
"Welcome to Death Row" - just waiting to die! Here now.
"They became pigs and they've become better Prisoners.
The Long arm of the Law decides on the style of sty ~
That's why Relationships are great, no need of lawyers
but they used that child as a Sledgehammer against You!"
"If Americans can't Park, they're not going...
that's what people want, 'Free Choice' ~ "
"Make a compelling, better Idea"

Golden Idols

"They think they're one with Them Selves ~
Not One with Krishna's Luminous Universe"
"She might have a Japanese Yakuza boyfriend
who likes big tattoos!" Nearly defeated by beauty.
It's coming out of her system. "She's bio-chemically
producing it. She lives with Synthetic hallucinations
not the Organic visuals; mushrooms, rare as Pearls.
The Cosmic Serpent ~ growing under a Guru's window.
"We form Governments and then let Them tell us how to live,
how to fornicate, contemplate, mate." Being multidimensional
Bridgeless ~ bridge

*

Glorious Kailash

*'Centre of the Universe' * Full bright, Moon festivals*
of Enlightenment. Another Cultural Revolution arrives!
Mandalas on fire, "What would you do for your friend?"
She took a Yak ride from Italy, through the Dromala Pass.
One with nature, Purely unpolluted, mia bella conneczione.
Less chatter in my Mind, the silence filled her with Potential.
"We've come so far away from what is natural ~
And we call this A.I. development, Progress!"
Discovering the honesty of Golden Profunda.

*

Mavericks

It's about catching the wave, slower, bigger waves,
riding their given faces ~ "I'm Right, You're Wrong!"
"Friday went to the Taj Mahal with a slave called Pussy"
"Really happy without it; War and human trafficing!"

*

Swami Resigning

"Life is just (too) funny ~ illusion's illusions", Shiva firing.
"What to do" 'Shanti Goa or Thai kick boxing your orbs?'
Simply enjoying in the heart light of Anjuna

Blooming Diamond Chakras at Manasorovar
Compassion's Lake, my Mind' s quiet, not thinking incessantly!
Prayer flags blowing over Lhasa city, Potala spiritual elevation.
At the highest altitude, bongs, bells, chanting, mantra sounds.
Serene elation of "Om Mani Padma Hum", telepathic ringing.
Girlfriends, got to let it happen ~ that's what you're doing;
being Open in a Lotus, give & take, feeling her Magicness
in purest, Prana dhamma. What great conceptions to carry
in your Heart, Chakra ~ May they unite in the Minds of All.
Living poetry, MahaYantras & Mandalas of still, calmness.
Creating Peace, Sacred Mindfulness of the human Spirit.
Samsara's dreaming in Ulan Bator. Circles of life & death.
No evils to corrupt the 'Mind' ~ from beyond is super clarity.
People built Stupas for the bones of many murdered Lamas.
No more Illusions, delusions; they're dead, "Chelo the body!"
"Communist bullets through the backs of their heads" -Genocide!
Chinese proverb, 'Man is born to die, woman is born to give birth'.

*

Public Obscenity Is being Naked
Default code, hereditary territory of Sufi trance memory.
Fine lines of Obsession, transparency as 'Cling film'
She's lying with her arse and brains smashed ~
in the bulldozed, rose garden of a modern Safi!

*

Lyrics to War & Glucose biscuits
Attention! Your patterns of your free flowing, growing ~
Seeds in the fields, sweet mangoes or bitter tasting Nim?
"Intelligence doesn't mean lack of psychosis sweetheart"
"It's alright Mara, I'm only bleeding from the Soul."
Instinctual, why like this? Are you their Guinea pig?
"On the bus or Off the bus" again, found my ripped-up ticket!
*'Possession is 9/11ths of the Law' ~ not to these Symbolists **
A delegation of Allegations from bloody, Autocratic Alligators.
The more obvious it becomes, always something vying for us…

<u>Keeping Cosmic Serpent's Spirit Alive</u>
*"The term Schizoid refers to an individual, the totality of whose
experience is split in two main ways: in the first place there's a
rent in his relation with his world and the second, there's a
disruption of his relation with himself. Such a person is not able to
experience himself together with others or at home in the world, but
on the contrary he experiences himself in despairing aloneness and
isolation; moreover he does not experience himself as a complete
person but rather as 'Split' in various ways, perhaps as a Mind more
or less tenuously linked to a body, as two or more selves and so on."*
R D. Laing. *'The Divided Self'*
*

<u>Satthipatana Sutra & Tao of Synchronicity</u>
*Amazing what we can achieve when we are Confident
and learn what not to do next time ~ but probably will!
If you still need to see the bullet holes in the wall, go to
Berlin, Santiago or Srebrenica; human, cannibal genes!
Being more Shanti inside yourself, 'Omkar ex-streaming'
Keeping the Perfect balance ~ manifestation of Shiva*
Shakti ~ Cosmic Myth is still True & Real in India today!
Understanding at many, many levels *Jung's Archetypes.
Everything in existence, everything is actually possible and
Shiva's infinite dancing with Parvati. Love that Ideally, whether
you click on it or not, is practicable again. Travelling through
Aquarius she always comes out on Top. Romantic, the nicest,
happy ride, getting what she wants! Organised, Programmed,
Conditioned, Unified Europa! Keep a natural vibe not Artificial.
You work through reality, real as any bubble, Consciously.
Roots of Grand commitment, only to a Powerful, Ego trip.
Have a great time travelling to any village on the Planet…
Legal exploration not exploitation; orgies of scarlet berries,
lovely banana custards, at a railway station in Rajasthan.*

Matisse's Friend

The paintings are your view, harmonies in colour ~
You know. Most people don't seem to have a clue!
What to do? Energetic experimentalists…
that would be the free flow

*

Pilgrimage to Gangotri by way of Leopards

'Maya' ~ "It's Meant to be, Really fucking Scary!!!"
Makes you want to Pray! And you Got to mean it!
"Please, Please, Please, God let me survive!"
Repeating the mantra and its Magic; it works!
Trying to catch the intensity in the eyes ~

*

Synthesising Spiked!

Idiot, You can't have the masses being illuminated; bleep!
Ergot made it all illegal and hardcore; Predators out stalking…
Salem's masses, unknowingly, munching on mouldy Rye bread!
Hallucinations ~ bypassing filters, Fully Opening Into the Universe!
Free to Party * Consciousness; condemned by Law, as Conspiracy!
Burnt at the stake, putting 1 & 1 together, trapped in an evil heresy!
Selective breeding turning plebs into dumbed-down sheep. Bo Peep!

*

Bonus Intimacy

Married a niece of Kali in Mali, painted by a Daliesque
Ingénue. Opening more of those Portals of Perception.
Of course, they're going to put a lock on the house!
Who is really living it ~ * ~ to Party, to be Truly FREE?
"With alcohol you don't need a lock…
because You can't get out of the room!"
Breaking the taboos, biological incentives.
I'd rather have a bullet in the head…
No, I don't know about that!
Whatever Sells doesn't mean it's Good!
He's gone into the water ~

Hot night in Tangier with Burroughs' gamine
"His writing was like an Atomic explosion, distortion in a Black hole!"
Wild Pear shape opportunities, on a fenny drip; DMT. Naked Lunch.
A billion times shrooms and an Alien! Crashing into a Sea of flowers
*

Cracks in the Sky
"You see this person in total panic ~
a sandwich isn't going to do anything!"
"A woman's best friend is the 'Revengence' Vibrator"
Aarh! "Darling everything's fine, I'm in Love with you again".
Sailing together by the full Moon across a Melanesian lagoon.
*

Fresh Felatio Recommended in Primavera
Weaving World, 'coitus interruptus' in ruby vortices.
Existential, nihilist, alchemist, no cause, no planning,
random arrival of the stranger in your perplexed face!
Read 'The Killer Inside Me', 'POP1280', 'Savage Night'
If we could only see it ~ soils, the earth, Zen country girl.
Giving your sweet mangoes from under trees of devotion.
Pure Rastafarian ~ living in the here and now continuum.
Awareness, observation of what your limited Mind's feeling
*

Blk & White always smiling
Living in hope, full colour, wearing garlands of Marigolds.
A delicate, golden brocade on your brightest, scarlet sari.
Beauties coming to kneel in front of someone like Buddha ~
Sunrise, Nile green eyes, ecstatic, happiness inside her cries
*

Ego-Syntonic Atomic
Wheatgrass is next best thing to blood; Life feeds off life,
the human Conscience of something Cosmic ~ changing.
Gonna put morality onto it ~ have another nice day soon.
The establishment believe in their elitism, superiority and
a servile population's inability to psychologically criticise!

NATURAL PSYCHEDELIC CONSCIOUS

There is no Narcissistic face to Buddha only Loving Kindness.
Vibes telling it as it is, not as the Ego-Me, cognitive dissonance.
Simply sharing, no chipped ID. ask any Innocent heart.
Identity, memory embedded from eating an apple,
then feeling ashamed; they had to ~ wear clothes!
Sensations, kissing her breasts, writing Love songs.
'This mission is too important to undermine ~
It's becoming more important than Life itself!'
*

Uncut Holographic Meadow

World Bank, IMF ~ OCED, IDA, BIS. G8; a summit for whom?
It's not supposed to be like that, environmentalist ~ terrorist!
My friend the Paddler, paddles through the pristine straits
of St. Juan de Fuca ~ the formless bridge to the Baleines' realm.
Violence to animals looks unreal, like photoshopped Disney World!
They're going to kill our salmon, why don't we listen to Iceland?
A fuck You to India; Coca Cola bottles, lingham is in every hut!
Meth. heads landing whatever it takes to get through the day!
"She's gonna bring it over"
*

Mine Sign

"Something to find out, Your Moon is in Leo… waveforms ~
the ascendant of Virgo. What's the Topest, most Top Secret?
I believe in, life is what You want it to be ~ really, and does she?
Whose Philosophy is that, the ideology of a hippie?" "Life is what you
believe is what you deserve; beautiful Peace of wild, seditious Minds.
Maybe it's not, if you feel we've all been mass-hypnotised in a Matrix"
"Told the taxman, 'that I've spent half of it on a Divine Mission,
can't have it back". Time to take it from the Richest in the land!
Grin and bear it, "Me, I don't like going under any Label mate!"
"Aren't you feelin' the Trance?" "I'm tryin' to get some sleep!"
A Free Spirit ~ creativity needs breath

Danger Sign: They ate all the seagulls long ago!
Religion is Power, but "I don't dance, I trance."
God bless you. "What can you do in Chapora?
Sink to absolute rock bottom and still get respect!
You can get a house wherever you want, can't you?
But you can get the ignorant neighbour from Hell!"
Good dynamic processing, how do you ever know?
I'm convinced, "Be leaving on the first day of rains ~
Radiating Love's Happiness; Good, is it close to Goa?
"Jesus came to set the captive free from ignorant bondage"
Nothing's a straight line, Hoffman was peddling my Pineal
Grand Sprite. There'll always be casualties of causalities...
Abusing yourself, nature, how we use them, it's really pathetic.
Dragonflies, Sea horses; things which will eventually kill them.
Ambushed the worm of desire ~ hooked on a needle of Love!
No attachment, no Mind, nothingness ~

*
Mercurious Consequences
Hypnosis, one of the faces of the waves ~ Do as I tell you!
The Mind you had to catch ~ focus your attention to escape.
"We direct our own, selfie movies. I can't watch that amazing
sultry, seductive arse, gorgeous hips and thighs anymore!
We'll get on the Mothership; playing with her purring pussy.
Nice to think about or not, the range of human emotions.
Why wanting to insulate from it ~ Open up to everything"
*"It's always good to get Respect." No Moon * Full Moon.*
Lots of doors coming off their hinges on the flowing path ~
Exactly same same, butterflies effecting constellations, stars.
"I woke up as fresh as Daisy", it doesn't have to make sense.
Connected is fully disconnected in time and space ~ loose,
being liberated, is enlightened, is being able to be Aware ~
Looking at Mind Objectively ~ life is rebirthing Cosmically.

The Divine Rights of Angels!

Corrupted the whole system to suit themselves.
Interpreting the Law making them into Absolute Kings.
When I came out of the black years and for awhile…
It might have been even longer than that.
The Government is a Trustee of my estate.
I'm the Executor, beneficiary, I'm God's child.
The judge is working for the Crown prosecution, deception.
The Government considers you legally as a dead person.
Certified as a Slave ~ You come to life as a Living Man

*

Anonymous Midnight Surfer

Free falling, lying through their Official, narrative teeth.
These are the ones who get shot at dawn by a wall!
'Absence makes the heart grow fonder!' Bollocks!
You see the truth in her heart! What you doin' that for?
"Doin' exactly what I want to do; nothing, and I love it!"
"Gotta be careful, fall in Love and I'm toast!"
Taking our Attention from the Essential ~

*

Just an Idiot

Nearly drove me to the edge of Madness ~ Hallo!
The kid was singing the National Anthem at 7am.
"It's the name of a band, probably Prozac upped"
Lost the plough, buried the hammer and sickle in a nuclear bunker.
Only the Icon was Allowed ~ Controlling People's Minds and Souls.
An Unholy Alliance, Russian Orthodox Church and tyrannical Czars.
"Communism is dead, Capitalism is Rampant"- Long Live Corruption!
That's the Model they fed us, what's the Target then Mr. Truman!
Four divorces, lost four houses, Heart Attack, kidney failure!
Beggars know exactly how much ~ tolerance you have.
Try some Orgasmic, Unfathomable, Universal feelings.
A beautiful Experience

Vision * Quests

Ethereal Cosmos ~ in tune with Earth
Participation, everyone shares in the Akashi domain.
Macro-micro, remembering everything existing
from the furthest light year, white dwarf star
into the deepest dimensions of the heart.
Who has to pay for Joy?
You make your own reality, every moment
together, transmutation ~ Trance, free Party.
Coming out whirling in the moment, dancing
going back to her primal juices
*

China has a different outline = I Chinging

As soon as you're on that energy level ~
"everything will be fine, you'll make it if you try."
Magician, Sorcerer, Shaman of your own reality
because there's absolutely no Judgement.
No more material frame, final ego game.
Electromagnetic * biochemical changing ~
Born again from the polarities of ever evolving visions.
All Mind mirages, Identity, planes of mass manipulation.
We are organic cell patterns * only energy, nothing gets lost.
Instantaneously making love with you in a new dimension.
Time ~ crossing on the tides of eternity ~
"don't wait for No man" ~ Mass circulation
*

Same Differences * That Mind-Setting

About the Inspiration ~ sharing what I love to Infinity.
On your molecular journey. "do dodo do do do dodo do
have you seen her, have yu seen my baby, tell me
have yu seen her, I need my baby, have yu seen her?"
All comes down to Vibration, her vibration, the same one
as me; meet the Individuals ~ morphing and conditioning.
Pie in the Sky; down my neck, they know those ropes!

Freedom 55

You hang them in that game, drown those in a Cenote.
.0001% of pop. have control of the Earth ~ All the Powers.
When will common sense bring us to a point of realisation?
Those reptile$ take you and me, to Deadly, Beastly War!
Global Market economie$ not Glastonbury's green Tor.
We see Ourselves in each other, your face, eyes in mine.
Many people take on these energies ~ in slime or divine,
or All in one; allowing Y/ourself to be; who we truly Are.
Allowing to be Unconditionally Free, putting our Actions
there to light up the runway ~ Unconditionally, can't wait…
*Spirit of Love, Love Spirit * Spiritual Love existing Spiritually.*
You in the reflection of me, of us, in a Mayan, Celestial lake.

*

Goa @ Crystal Mantra

Inspiration to live it regardless, fearless, generous, gracious,
*dauntless, of Bombs, panjandrums, psy*ops, ego centralisms.*
"As soon as you look for you, you help yourself…
You help look for Mother Earth, you'll help her too"
A big gift ~ but it was just my imagination…
"Have to Love Yourself to Love Others"
And to be Free, Compassionately, just in Love"
Radiating in the moment ~ Relating <> Why not?*
"You can have relationships but just have to know ~
A dream come true, its changing as intrinsic flow"

*

Siesta * Fiesta

"Come Home, Pass Out"
"Spending Time with my pussy
Flowing with the Babaette ~
taking wheat grass, thinking about my health.
It was horrible, still had a bit of respect left.
Love your arse, gave her a Tick Tack."
She won't know the difference…

<u>Diamond Crown Chakra of Mother Earth</u>
'Human Adaptation', Indices, Personality is happening.
Our little self to one side ~ let the Spirit run in us.
Who's too scared of going in a box without another box?
Tell it like it is, baby, "Mrs Jones we got a thing goin' on."
I know deep down inside, I believe you Love me.
Letting Myself go, "where I am." Never leave me!
"He's leavin', leavin', on that midnight train…
*
<u>A very nice Smile ~ In the Heart</u>
To keep up that Level ~ seeding of Inspiration.
"Learning that dreams don't always come true."
Full power natural, Organic Magic Mushrooms!
Her divine, deep kissing, passionately arouses ~
*
<u>Never forget about the Illusion at the door</u>
Good Faith business ~ In Mercurial Cahoots.
*Release melancholic blockers * Vibe is metabolic Freedom.*
Replenishing the Serotonin pool ~ transmuting Spring days.
Just the nature of things, Invasions of greed, Ignorance, violence!
Transcendental pressure, for Illumination purposes, at the Tower.
Streams gushing, flowing; misunderstood, spreading the signals.
Elevators ~ of Your Mind > being as light as possible!
*
<u>My DNA Spell</u>
Giving them Circuses and bread and you can do what you want!
It's a fraud, embezzlement, deceiving people on so many levels!
It's a Form of black Magic from an invisible witch's hand.
Imagine sending hypnotic incantations around the world.
Casting global illusions, unreal, but everyone believes it.
Is everything pointing in the direction of Love ~ reality?
What we call society, culture is hanging by a thread.
I'm not like, "what's it all about?" ~ just a little smile.
A whole country recovering from Total devastation!

Dreamrithm
A new sort of Unrequited Love, You learn from everyone.
Happy with her memory, be happy inside wherever you are ~
His palm beach hut, Last Hippy Standing, lookin' at the Stars fall.
Biggest Secret, Secrets; MahaKali without her outstretched wings!
What's with you NSA? Got to be open to dark magic, Saturn's rings ~
Fall in Love, which is on our Minds; I think therefore It is, I am thinking.
It's all good, feeling, at least I'm able to have a thing, called a thought!
Descartes' devotees on the Ghats at Benares, burning a candle light!
Keeping the balance of waves crashing on the reef ~ a natural vibe.
The Island's perfumed breeze, gliding gently, softly through the air.

*

"God blessed me with You"
Crisis, another Tipping Point, a Typhoon of Schizoid Chaos!
Crocodile tears, hypocritical grief, haughty disdain, deceit.
Tranquil eyes * hers, of anxiety, stress and depression.
Being beyond the range, beyond the rage!
Transcending human experiences ~
Climb together, climb alone.

*

Corazones beating in heat!
'The Model', Represents ~ a representation.
LSD. be cool and there's a Vibe of Freedom.
Knowing how to flow with the grand Illumination,
knowing how to treat a sadhu's Italian Chillum.
Flooding tribal serotonin, on Aswem beach ~
Shiva Shakti, Super cool, super Nova Express.
"Keeping On & Om ~ being Conscious of Your Mantra"
Transcend thoughts, taboos, dogmas, formulae, Mind-Forms.
We are Cosmically, humanely, potentially more than any fear,
dream, hallucination, indoctrination, conditional sensation or ~
"I believe the Invisible hand exists". Roots and Extensions…

"The Best Is Yet to Come ~ It's here Now"
How to Live like that? Realise it's Mind's self-preservation ~
Just being In a Universe of Expectation with No Expectation.
Not even any acknowledgement from Someone You Loved!
Not the slightest, get your heart around that one! "As It Is."
Now tough to understand your responsibility in any of this!
*Reflecting the light source ~ light force * light course…*
Reworking my Merkababy on lit up sea cliffs, at sunset.
No more pundits, pandits, panjandrums, New Labour fakirs.
Living in a Sub Culture, not getting values; "As Seen On TV".
Authority to $ell you something, Ok. because its been on BBC!
Dumbed down, 'Global Hegemonists' with pocket Atom Bombs.
Welcome to Horror's nightmares, on us, wake up or perish!
A contract with the Devil, as seen, 'On the Lucifer Channel'.
Relative Values,You don't need to be from Grammar School,
an Escapologist, Anthropologist, Strategist, to Understand.
That if you Destroy my brother's home, (for Democracy!)
If you rape my sister and disrespect my daughter, son
I'll be Extremely, Extremely Unhappy. "Don't be Nasty!"
Be careful of 'The Outer Limits with no true just reason'
Making the Realisation; what You (We) want of Light.
Energies ~ to turn the Mind and Heart to Infinite Spirit.
Listening to what's coming ~ Precious Cosmic Temple.
*

The Diamond Cutter
It's Your Mind that Operates on the Mind ~
Overcome any defilements with clear breath.
Emancipation purification, pacification of Auxiliary Attacks.
But how to go < beyond > this Mind of yours inside Space?
Deeper penetration, concentration, awareness, salvation.
*Your Psy*trancing prayers at Shiva Valley, by the sea.*
Quieten ~ calmness of the nature of Infinity.

Schadenfreude's Black Hole of Grief
"There's no word in the English language
for a loving parent who has lost a child!"
Where did 'I' go wrong, 'I' don't know, really.
Damaged memories * lost her box of pleasure.
"Life is good, choose the happy path, treasure."
No beginning * No end, No fear ~Trusting.
"Here you can simply be yourself"
*
*

Box of blockers & disclaimers
"Chicas hissing in Ecuador
Head full of Coke ~
Quite the Ego trip!"
Marching Powder, brain drain.
*

Prone ~ Full Moon Chick
Prototype of Romantic Phallicies!
That's what people are predicting…
You've got to pay for your Protection.
Thank Your Lucky Stars crossing in the night ~
Alright, so we're on the perfect gleaming beam.
That's the main vibe * beautiful shanty dream.
Peace ~ harmony; Tolerance Not Ignorance.
How far will you go to let go ~ of Your Ego?
"Give me an Aspirin ~ I'm ready to go now!"
Working with the Universe, don't you see?
Always Fully Thinking of something else!
"Life Is Good ~ You can choose, free will
The Happy Path for sure" for one's destiny.
Being Possessive, Possessed of Nothing.
Flowing in Line -*- with the whole

"The day I set You Free!"
Had a stupid accident ~ she was right there too!
Synchronicity ~ of My action, a Universal disaster.
Real Protection of the Dhamma, being alive in Your Life.
Playing in Goa, not making their radiated, perpetual psychewars!
'Men of War', enslaving those Nobler Savages. Villagers' laughter,
carefree, playing on soft, crystalline, beaches and then one day ~
they, the conquerors invaded, wanting to claim it ALL; didn't they?
Research & Development technology; unbelievable competitiveness!
That same potential is used to sell us Unhealthy food, fluoride;
to send Prisoners to countries which have no Human Rights,
to be Tortured, 'Legally', by what means we can't Imagine!
These Futuristic Super Hi-Tech/AI/Science Resources are
used to exploit, to Manipulate, to destroy life, humanity and
our Planet's environment for greed! They are fully capable to
use their toxic set of unholy tools to secure, feed false Needs!
Spiritual, Free Spirit over Mind over Matter. What's it all mean, natural
ecstasy? "Life Is Good." Take a deep breath, Prana, next breath in ~
out ~ changing next beat, in ~ out, vision in front of my eyes ~ now
*

Decoupling their Absolute Programs
*Naturally ~ **HEART**HEART**HEART**HEAR**THEART**HEART*
What you feel is more important than what you think.
"Whatever the official narrative is don't believe it."
Surrounded by scientists with systemic answers?
Digital cybernation, look the other way; You will never know!
System Inflexibility, dragging us all away from our true Nature.
Trans-human robots' exposure to a patent, plastic-cup planet.
How you gonna find out who you really are in all of this illusion?
ENOCHIAN Magic sitting in a hemp Pentagram beside Maya.
Paying filmstars fortunes to distract us, getting all our attention.
Getting away with cruel genocide, crimes against our Humanity!
Everything is a manifestation, an incantation of limited Mind-ego ~
Creating beyond many different things ~ as omnipresence is Space

Relationship *Observing * Objectively * Re*evolving
A Live plant has spirit, has Prana, holistic Life force.
No Fear > Memories of the Black hole, again & ~
The Refuge > free of (being bonded to) the Wheel.
Ever turning, whatever comes ~ try and let it flow.
"Your Mind is Your Best Friend or Worst Enemy."
Seeing a Part of the Mind ~ keeping concentration,
breath, as a Technique, becoming Aware of Mental-
thoughts that make it behave, operate in such ways!
How to make it more recognisable, so we are aware of
how it Operates on Us, making us React in such & such
ways > becomes obvious after a while, with experience,
having to deal with it in innumerable situations ~ calmly.
It's truly amazing but once you see its building bricks ~
respect its devilish tricks! To feel its own Self's-Creation.
How to be able to study the Mind, our ubiquitous thoughts,
when we are constantly caught up within its Magic delusions.
How to see, witness it for what it truly IS, without Negating it!
Shiva with a Cobra round his neck, no ego, fearless, in control,
through full Awareness, as a Charioteer driving the wild horses!
Knowing the correct contexts, concepts of Mind is Important.
Using Mind, to become Consciousness, of whole Mind, Itself.
Becoming aware of its Karmic response as bodily sensations
flowing freely, non-attached, in tune, resonating with inner streams.
Structuring a Conscious tool, not being a wild elephant or monkey.
Penetrating to the subtlest depths, the Universe within & without.
In the sub-Atomic fields of body-Mind, arising & passing away
through equanimous observation of these changing sensations.
Trying to Realise change ~ these habit patterns of the Mind-sets.
Being tuned up with it, the causes of our blind reactions; now ~
"We're totally at the whim ~ of our sensory Input, stimuli."
Causes, Reaction, Conditioning > Awareness, 'Identify'.
Cosmic Contact as the basis of human mental content ~

This Is It

Can we ever go with the flow or is it a wild goose chase ~
putting them all to the Illusory, finitely edged, unholy sword?
No anger, Heart; time is ticking away, ever changing patterns.
*See clearly beyond sectarian boundaries, to inside * no outside.*
Same same Transcendental reality, no more Technique, as It Is.
It's the Mind that Operates on the Mind, Our Ego-Mind-thoughts
makes us think, believe this, 'Is Who we are', totally, not relatively.
What is it Inside, the roots, the influences, our own seeds of Suffering.
Ignorance, Illusion, Pain, desire, expection, freedom, all the delusions.
Liberation, how to witness Self for what it truly is, its mystical character,
Illuminated nature of Self-Creation, flowing sub-consciously, to be alive.
Using Mind to Penetrate, Understand, Its own thinking-Self-limited-Mind
Accept it for just what it is, as No-Self manifesting in the Space of now.
Infinitely boundless, not negating but embracing it All, without judging!
Altruistic love absorbing, reflecting all sensations, experience of true life.
Conscious of continuously changing habit patterns, realising, no ego ~
*

Cultivation of the 'Brahma Vihara' Garden

Metta, the highest Feeling towards all beings ~ highest vibrations.
*Attain Inner * Outer Peace together ~ Buddha's dhamma teaching.*
The Predators are expelled! Thank fuck for that, bunch of maniacs!
Peace, no war or war over a family's disputed possession of a River?
"Is it of more intrinsic value flowing with water or your family's blood?"
No Wars were created on behalf of dhamma, becoming calmer ~
Peace, Impartiality, friendliness to All, from bathing in the waters
of Loving Kindness, Compassion, Sympathetic Joy, Equanimity.
Conquest Is Spiritual Not Political, Egoic, Economic or Military.
"Victory breeds hatred, the conquered sleep in deep sorrow ~
cast aside victory and defeat. A Peaceful one dwells at ease.
Hatred does not cease by hatred, hatred ceases by Love."
'Dhammapada'

*'Ahimsa'- Completely Selfless, boundless, multi*dimensional,
compassionate, the concept of a friend, Openness, Oneness.
'Altruism to All the World Systems, All the Earths, Suns, Moons,
Oceans, Galaxies, Universes, Infinite Milky Ways, alive inside.
Hinduism's Action > Concept of society, of Caste, Life
given in 'Divine Sanction'. As being a Creation of God!
Gotama's discovery of a new, Evolutionary dynamic'.
"Fatherhood of God, implies the brotherhood of man!"
What's this Feeling ~ a/part of the Mind? This Thinking...
Control of What, Why? Mind-sets, Mental-illusory games.
'Each one's duty is to help his fellow beings, Mother Earth.
The equality of the one species of mankind; sharing it All'.
'Loving Kindness' is based on this 'Oneness' ~ Openness
because, All people are capable of the Highest Spiritual
Attainment, beyond limited Intellectual Understanding ~*
*
*'Do Not Feed the Animals'
"If we raise the Vibration we'll see the Truth"
'That sweet Heart who went through Hell for you!'
Superiority, frame of Mind, living with a fascist mosquito.
"Sometimes People Need Fear!" Food used as a Weapon!
'Hooked or not, into the Machine' said my environmental,
Activist Friend, 'don't need secret nerve gas experiments,
nor Uranium 239, plutonium 242, radioactive birth control'
Foetuses screened for determining the Pre-crime of their family.
Threats to a Global elite; needs sterilisation, eugenics' programs.
Selective breeding, more advanced to dominate the Common man.
Revolt of the plebs', bad gene pools, their rebelious, child-database.
Let's have a proxy war, being a sponsor of inhuman attrocities!
"Happiness is a gift, not to expect it but to delight
in it and to add to other people's store of it"
Living the Ideal moment ~ what a beauty!
Extinction of the cock ups*

WavyGravy ~ Again&Again&
Streams of Consciousness passing
through Your Mind-state reflection ~
*

Shiva*Shakti
"Are you a Slave?"
"To share Love ~"
*

Big Sur * Revolution
"Only replaces one Jackass with another Jackass"
'One Power with another Power'
"One for me and One more for me!"
That's why we need another ~ Renaissance.
Skeptics getting the proof of an Albino Redwood.
*

Timeless Perpetual Creation
There's aaalways a War goin' on ~ It's the Image!
"The thing is to be Constant, not always Correct."
Pipe dreams, head above the clouds, embracing PachaMama.
"Breaking the Mould! There is no Mould; drop the projector!"
"I'm Working on my Streaming ~ Collective Unconscious"
*

Holy Pope 'fuckin' Innocent' No good for nerves or hysterics!
"Hey Bunny we're goin' to the Men's Colony", You mean prison?
"Sheep bow down to the God they put in front of them"
"Something more than your own Life ~
truly facing Your death with Love"
This plot has a global dimension. Ask a dervisher.
#UNRIG, "Fear is the Ultimate Weapon of Control"
"Do you know what will happen?" * "No, it was a feeling!"
What are drones good for? Too late the US. Cavalry's arrived!
Free of the Palace, another Anonymous 'serfer' kicks the bucket!
Asleep, taking all they can get their hands on, perfectly unconscious.
No threat to a psychopath. Would you like to meet the Sultan of hearts?

Clearly Simplified Complexities ~ Brands on both sides
'Some Sense of Meaning'- "All Humans are animals; contact!"
Sent fundamentalists to spread 'faith', Indoctrinate the natives
with an Ideology of Ancient Holy, Insanity. Militants ignoring
Rational Science but feeding divine, murderous, Intolerance.
'Axis of evil, virus of our Planet. US. UK. Israel, Saudi Arabia!'
Attacking the Houses of Innocent childhood with Hellfire!
Labeling Children with Religions of Pastorised Parents.
Unaware of Conditioning, divisions of Identificationings.
Why the Segregationings? Creating roots of racist devils.
Your kids need to see, http://howtheworldreallyworks.info/
"Need to profess a healthy Ignorance for the whole Universe"
"Your dinner's in the oven lad."
*
Your Nat Raja Jaguar
Space ships up there, we came out of the same box!
Shooting stars, constellations, all encompassing all ~
Make me a Vicadin Martini, Bunny ~ brakes are tight.
Perfect ride to Bolinas going from Stop to slow to Go.
There goes that Brain again, on a painted Thunderbird.
Shoot that Lion, trap that bear in your razored snare!
Don't make eye contact, just Power Walk on by ~
Hezbollah Insurance agents all seen as bad brokers.
"But Our 'Good Guys' only directed their Activists!"
*
At the Inn of Dervishes Don't Abuse Your Self
Breaking the Mould >< realtly, here is No Mould!*
Really we create our Own Moulds. Heart's calling.
OK, I tuned into OCD; Obsessional Consequences.
"I've got the brain of a young, sweet Bridget Bardot!"
Any Blonde Bombshell; sexism with brains to booty!
Pleasing your Lover not Psychological Coercion.
"If we raise the Vibration we'll know the Truth"
Freeing myself of my thoughts and doubts

Unmasked Cruiser

"Side tracked ~ with a Limbo dancer, silent partner.
Can't lie to genetics or escape your Self's chemistry.
Living in a gerbil factory, overcome with more grief,
pull your head out of your ass. Here we go again...
I have better things to waste my time on"
'Eternity is a long life ~ now, when you connect
to yourself, you're connected to everything here.'
Why condemn it out of hand? It's a Rip Off right?
Most of them sucking it all in. Ah well what can you do?
Caught carrying that secret viral, chemical mix in a coke can.
What will they charge them with, intent to blow up a Jumbo?
Their Full On Mind Games, Yu kidding me; Oh, Yeah, Really!
The event created Maximum disruption for 100,000 hapless people.
Motives of maimed moslem insurgents carrying shampoo bottles.

*

Filme Très Noir

To track his moments ~ from Pope Urban's call for a holy,
1st crusade, to Massacring the unbelievers, in the nursery!
Another World Reality is completely subjective, your holiness.
"Don't get assassinated for throwing stones, throw Pine cones!"
They were here first; bears armed to the teeth at the Trail head.
Long death march from canyon palaces of Chaco, New Mexico.
His c.v's, 'the time we went to Vegas and did acid for three days'
Who's the bigger chimp? Not just anyone can become a martyr ~
Dreams come true, she always wears beautiful, iridescent saris.

*

Dodging the bullets, biting the bullets

Don't take it personally, 'Anicca'. "Fuck You", a demon sliding ~
round pegs into square holes of neuroses, within bodies of time.
Passing through the Pain barrier's contractions ~ expansions.
'Oneself is more powerful than our enemy', Rumi...
Breathing sparkling, transcending, waves of sensations.
Seeing myself in the mirror of my Lover

Says he's enjoying what's goin' on Inside his head
Another Army's toxic dose of, 'DO OR DIE! Don't Stop!
These People are living under a Massive Microscope ~
Not another line to complain about, whining pommes.
Revolutions, U N. Resolutions, Agenda 21 ~ Ad Infinitum.
It's like drunken pornography; a useless wanking shop.
Not even understanding the basic causes of the roots ~
Always leading up to another 'Massacre of The Innocents!'
Jews in the News, Jew rues Salaam, Zionists in holiest Bedlam.
Anti-Semite, igniting the dynamite, minus Insight not very bright!
Caught up in a vortex, a twist of fate, Chimping 'till it's too late…
Not bothered about Heaven; Hell, definitely don't want to go to!
What the, 'bleep' do you do now Abraham? Sacrificing a child!
All Perfect just needs to be revealed; why's it so concealed?
Don't need to know or do anything Really ~ just changing.
I'm not just anyone's martyr, took the wrong worm hole…
ended up in LA. with a plastic Koran, ready to blow up
The Magic Mountain, Wham, Bam!
*

Recipe on: How to Make Love
(Read the manual!) 'How to Make It Amazing'
Stops it happening ~ from going Pear shaped!
'Consume Obey Submit'- Royal Tattoo on a cog.
Noble to conscientiously object, Cosmic Subject.
"They knew I would allow my Conscience to do ~
what's right." Which part did my Mind play in this?
"Newton's laws on Motion came from a contract
with the Navy, for better gunnery!" Sorted that then!
Transfixed throughout with Life, resonating Crystals ~
Picked up the DDT. pesticides for another perfect day!
'From mother's milk in Finland and in the fat of Penguins'.
"My chemicals are going back to Gaia * Immersing with it"
Into Pure flame. "Daisies regulating their own temperature"
Absorbing ~ reflecting Sun light for Earth's balancing act

*Not just a selfish gene * Just hard wired to survive*
Gases for 3½ billion years from plants, self regulating
Organisms, Control the Atmosphere, oxygen of the World.
Self Creation ~ Interest of a Greek Earth Goddess, Gaia.
Passing through the edgy darkness of far Stratospheres.
Avatars raising Awareness in people's veiled, blinded minds!
Can't let the electricity go off for a week without panicking,
taking us back into ancient realms, dystopian Testaments.
Science, foods and fuels, revelations of a new Apocalypse!
"Not just life but the whole system"
Becoming very True!
*
Aeroflop - Stepping on a Sacred Scarab
Defiling impulses in a State of tension and unrest.
The Master desire ~ what's the Ultimate score?
Nothing's for sure, burnt to the core, red f… raw.
Third eye's open I saw, Monkey people, unto law.
"Of Karma of Action, is a Reactionary correlation.
Nirvana's not a 'Conditioned' causal experience."
Unconditioned, uncaused, timeless ~ located beyond,
Mind-thoughts, transcended ~ inner space mon amour...
Conditioned, possessing free will; attainment of freedom ~
forever. Sublimation and deconditioning not reconditioning.
Causal processes directed, 'understood by the logical-mind'.
And Individual, moral responsibility for justice in the Universe?
Witness this Mind, develop Spiritual vision of direct experience ~
*findings of these explorations * fractal, holograms, regenerations.*
'Belief that War is a lesser evil to being dominated by an opponent',
said Black Elk. If goodwill is present, for those who love humanity
more than themselves, unilateral disarmament without the fear of
genocidal consequences; working for Pacifism, is truly possible ~
Mindfulness-mindlessness, conscious, take your pick, do your best.

<u>Charge of Heart * Change of System</u>
*"The noblest victor is he who would conquer himself rather
than defeat a 100,000 men in battle."* Dhammapada 103.
*"Conquer enmity with amity, evil with good, conquer miserliness
with charity and falsehood with truth."* Dhammapada 222
*Conquest through Dhamma, not extremely, painful slaughter!
Devotion to a Universal Monarch, Full Heart, Supreme Space.
A being's salvation lies in one's own hands ~
Come in as a caterpillar ~ go out as a butterfly*
*

<u>Good Luck Shack's Pot Holes</u>
*Irrational, abstract, Indians can't drive straight ~
Even at night, surreally weaving alone on the road.
From where are the Powers making us so Fear full?
Giving no trust; needs full homeopathic, bright people.
Signals through a nervous system, rooting the illnesses.
Repairing brain sub-conscious ~ on special frequencies.
Electro-magnetic meridians * fully working energy fields.
Ions, electrons, channels, nerves, working the Life force ~
Immune system falls how long when cleaning your teeth?
How much waste Aluminum is there hiding in the fluoride?
Obelisks to Power the eagle of War, in another austerity Crisis!
Ubermensch, threw lots of missiles, sold a Hell of a lot of bombs!
How clever they are or how stupid we are; Conspiracies R4 Real!
Such sophisticated control techniques of what we truly don't know;
And what we think we do know. Super vega testers & Adbusters.org
EMF. manipulation of the circuit wires, transmitters, receivers, WIFI.
'300 billion processes happen in the body each second ~
Aiding biological warfare, being smaller than a cell within a cell.
We need clear filters, honesty, Integrity for rejection, reaction!
'This amendment is about transparency and more openness'
Take your pick, modern hippies ~ Opening with will power.
Life goes up and down but you don't have to ~ Be LOVE.
From the beginning of time, always been people dancing.*

Cosmic Oceanic

'Working as a light being, I am the light'. Heart is courage.
"If no fear, no need of Politics or of Pseudo-Governments"
'America is being bankrupted.' "here the Time is Now ~
get the solar Spaceship ready, rev-up the mercury cells.
Spiralling of Merkaba's, multi*dimensionality*Vibration.
"If it's meant to be; You're meant to be in Shiva's India".
A house needs love, needs people. Karmic iambic…
Channel its response ~ Earth ascending, extra-sensory,
meaning, full <:> less ~ Allowing one's own experience.
Sitting silently, still in the Heart
*

Maha Yantra at the Anonymous Images Showbar

There's more emotional women with more logical, stronger men!
How to move beyond our boundaries; addictions and obsessions?
It is what it is it is ~ defining something as, 'Wrong Love'.
Realise Realisation ~ Fear is Fears > dreamers dreaming.
Intellectually seems, all in the Mind, My Mind and emotions!
All comes back ~ all exists for that moment of 'Surreality'
Cracked - the neural coding and Gut reaction, feelings of
sensations on the body, in Mind, from the Sub-Conscious,
working on those seeds blooming in the fields of reaction ~
Awareness of this (5 Aggregates, Nama*Rupa) Processing.
Narcissism in tune, less gloom* light as balloons on a Moon,
floating all the way to golden, shimmering, Brahma Viharas.
On Parami Jetstreams, in precious atmospheres of full loving.
Loving kindness, compassion, sympathetic joy and Equanimity.
Sure you can interact with Love more Lovingly, sweetest Baby.
The deep attachment of the Ego, the same in 528 BC as Now.
How do you leave your wife, your husband, and your children?
A basis of relationships, took dips in relative, swirling streams ~
Swimming in knowing, not drowning in crypto, auto-expectation.
Takes one lover to destroy another, destroying themselves.
Life's lessons, giving Metta, not loving in a vacuum flask.

Islam: from Arabic 'aslama', submission, resign oneself,
from Syriac, 'aslem' to make peace, surrender; derived
stem of slem, to be complete (see slm in semitic roots).
*

Avatar Gallery -'Allah means One God'
Let's all go on an esoteric cruise with Muhammad & Ali.
"The door of Love is always open." I Like that…
'Channelling embodies one's vastness ~
'the flower of Life' derived from a photon belt vortex…
with enneagrams holding I Chings and gold Merkabas.
Wants nectar of Immortality not invitation to the Bilderbergs!
Path to theTemple of Love at Atlantis, with ascending angels.
'Dejeuner sur l'herbe' ~ Living is Life's only purpose ma Cherie.
Enjoying a lovely picnic in the garden of Sri Nisargadatta Maharaj
*

Waves in Space
Streams of consciousness
passing through your Mind
continuously ~ effortlessly
*

Ohming
Om Sweet Om ~ suffusing, dissolving.
8,300,000 + hits for *Psychedelic Art*
Welcome to the Amazing Universe of Alex Grey.
"If it works it's obsolete." Marshall McLuhan.
"The American Media has a way of imposing
Its own assumptions on the unwary"
*

Euclid's Meniscus
FULL POWER *FULL FEELING* FULL FLOW
burning out * bowing out.
Smiling in fear and the
Cultivation of grace ~

Hieroglyphic Pareus

Lunar reversing; I Like Expansion ~ Manifest expansion,
expansion expansion expansion expansion, contradiction.
Contraction is expansion ~ spiraling around in a Fibonacci
sequence; living Pictographs inside a golden ratio Pyramid.
"When you make it mean whatever you want it to mean."
Found the Love of Your Life; downloaded the Love of a Wife.
In the tiniest, green grass thong, a gorgeous, naked Tahitian.
Saw a lot of shooting Star constellations, multi*dimensions.
One in your crystal eyes (Cosmic hologram).

*

Next Right

'University of Judaism', brain washing American Lobbies.
Why do you believe the USA. is 'misunderstood' outside?
Yeah, spinning with Negative propaganda from like, CNN.
"Because nobody focuses on the Real people here" at Fox.
Politics and Entertainment does an Injustice to America ~
As soon as they got off the boat, they said, "This Is Mine!"
"All Mine, You are a Slave, you now belong to me and my God!"
"News at the top of the Hour" ... Back to, 'This week at War'.
Media control and domination of the Truth for Neo-Fascism.
Continuously showing War, catastrophe, us under attack -
Mind-set, Wind Up, Mind up, Pre-eminent in Power-Mad!
"The Station with the Most Trusted Name in News" Yeah!
"I wasn't raised in an insane War so that was a good thing"
Other people kicking down your door, invading your space.
Leaving home at 3am going to school. Threatened from
Cold war communists to New fundamentalist, terrorists!
No mistakes possible now ~ You're Under Attack! Again!
"When you see what people could do, with all that money
for the betterment of us all, it's Amazing!" No foresight ~
"Pass the bullets and praise the Lord!" I'd make a terrible
War Photographer. Time I got the camera out of the bag,
another Tomahawk would have gone by

Trippy dot the 'I's
'The place no one knew', sitting in a park in Sozopol
waiting for the Italian futurists. Bella…
Project Prospect Perfect Respect Reflect
"Wilderness must be preserved ~ it is a Spiritual, open backdoor,
a safety valve for those who never enter them."
Still water's golden reflection in a crystal, clear lake
Is a natural Symbol

*

Violet light in a Lava Mind
I never had enough evidence before to say to it,
"to go!" ~ Over them - disconnect, leave me with
the Cosmos, Peace and Loving kindness.
Embracing the new connections of reality,
signs of evolution, nothing is rejected ~
Resonating, creative parts of light force
focusing on, Protecting Mother Earth.
Projecting spectrums of infinite energy.
Contact to fiery Phoenixes of Inspiration.

*

Someone who comes out of nowhere
Let it go ~ who really cares, really?
Keeping the frequency ~ levels up.
Good for the business
Good for the energy.
Who cares?

*

Jigsaw Puzzle
Exchanges of energy ~
Changing of the Kali Yuga of true Space.
How to make the World a Happier Place.
People trusting, being in the moment ~
Now I'm not going back
going with the flow ~

Suma's Astral Projection
Drama Baba Boom, in Charas*land…
A Zen-thing, what the fuck happened?
'He was a prophet in his own land'
Not that I'm anti-hippie * on the trippier side.
"A pot of ghee's more important than money
And everybody would eat...."
*

"I say Bless her"
The girls, Wow can they dance, Pussy enslaved.
"Just keep 'em comin', I'll tell you when to stop!"
"Why not do today what you can do again tomorrow?"
You can't hide anywhere… who wants to be found?
Baggage, 'they lose their fluffiness' sparkling radiance.
Being in Love * You see that happiness, glowing inside.
'Try to be an angel and make someone smile'
*

Insatiable * Unsociable
Banks… payin' in the f…..g ass.
In a World of buying and selling people, children!
'To live is nothing, to whom does this world belong?'
Dealing with insanity with a gun! Automatic trigger…
She learnt it all in jail, becoming more self-radicalised!
Shiva Space * 'Sorry, I've been dancing here for 20 years,
Fuck Off!'
*

Be aware of the dog
Golden Nataraj is gliding; always excused by Vested Interests!
You a subject; Obey their Commands, while Worshipping them.
Using formulae of the Third Reich to Control Hearts and Minds.
We Believe the MATRIX is so Real
that we disconnect with Life Itself ~
Dramatic ~ it's just an intense story.
Underneath it all Is eternity

Space Vision
The Human Body-Mind-Contact Mission…
'CONDITIONING' Ultimately, doesn't exist.
We are alone, we know we're alone, so ~
We're totally
* Connected *
Totally connected
And totally Unique
*

Specks of Smartdust
The light we all have ~
Star Cellular Rainbows
We're definite, infinite infinity.
I always like that Zero point.
Streaming Consciousness ~
*

Intuition
Being in the Heart
Mind is still active
we are now ~
in this integral moment
the rest is of Ego stuff…
Who's caring even sharing?
But we don't buy into it…
Becoming other Inspiration
Keeping in this moment ~
Intuiting the Bigger Picture.
Sharing primary essence
Ultimately letting it all go.
Being happier, letting it flow ~
Letting my Mind think like this.
Refocus, glowing with the flow
with the flow, flow flow ~

The Independent, London, August 1st 2006
'New Classification of Drugs Table.'
Being Aware of Illusion (Maya Mind). Everything is a Meditation…
*'The House of Commons Science and Technology Select Committee
Condemns the existing illegal drug classification system, saying it's
based on 'ad hockery and conservatism' and should be scrapped.
It proposes replacing it with a whole new scale that would rate
substances purely on the basis of health and social risks involved
in taking them. Systems now don't tell us how dangerous or not ~
the drugs actually are. "The present approach owes more to Fear
than to reason." It would also make it more immune from cynical
Political grandstanding. Britain's antiquated drugs' laws stand
accused of failing millions of people because they bear little or no
relationship to the harm caused by everything from a hit of heroin,
to a seemingly harmless pint of lager. The Home Office has been
advised by its own senior advisers that alcohol and tobacco are
more harmful than the class A drugs of LSD and Ecstasy.
"This shows why we need a radical overhaul of the current
classifications which are riddled with anomalies and clearly not
fit for purpose." Copies of the report have been submitted to the
Home Office which has failed to act on the conclusions'. Obviously.*

*

*"What is the Intention, Use?" ~ 'Path with the Heart'
Context: DNA. sacred synchronistic marriage ~ Tao in the now
Raising the frequency, clearing the Karma, Spirit re*birthing the
Levels of Truth. Channeling Powers of the moment ~ Mysticism
and Quantum Physics. How to use the LSD. key to Open
the Universal Consciousness.'The Doors of Perception'
Not Obsessional, Painful Addictions, Reactions. Be Wise ~
And how much coffee can you handle? How much do you
Unconditionally Love your Life and wife, the planet and humanity?
Drugs have a natural tradition of relieving pain & being Shamanic.
'Tune In, Turn On, Drop Out'*

The mantra of the 1960's 'hippie, social, cultural revolution'.
Paradigm shifts into the 'Age of Aquarius', new insights into
'Multi-dimensionality*Reality' ~ Meditation is my Connection
to the Universe", to recognising the Matrix of my finite Mind.
'Easy Rider' 'Woodstock' 2001, exploration of Outer Space ~
'Landing on the Moon' 1969! Now Discoveries of Inner Space.
Use of Psycho-Active drugs, the 'Global village', new Sensitivity
to your Lover * your child and to Mother nature. Awareness of
different cultures and their philosophies. LSD. a Super Catalyst
that's been suppressed by Governments from the 1960's, Why?
Look at the information in this table, is this another conspiracy?
The multi-billion dollar War on a $ multi-billion 'illegal/legal' drugs,
Global Industry. Dr Timothy Leary, judged, 'The Most Dangerous
Man In America' Why? Politics to Control the Individual, people's
potential to be more Consciously Aware and live together, sharing
different values, perceptions? "As the person who's taken LSD. for
the longest period are there any physical side effects?" "None, you
lose synapses, of which you have trillions." This table finally helps
clarify the brain-washing on what is happening to our human rights!
Senior Government advisors warned that Alcohol and tobacco are more
dangerous to the Nation's health than Class A drugs, LSD and Ecstasy.
However one drop of Acid is NOT less, than having two Vodka cocktails
or smoking a pack of 'American Spirit' my friend. Be Aware that LSD. 25
has the Potential to open windows into different multidimensions and to
take you to places you cannot imagine. As DMT; it is a Super powerful
Catalyst and has to be treated with Love, Full Respect. If taken well,
Consciously, no overdosing, there should be amazing, real Insights.
People 'trip' each day in these ever changing fields of Psychedelia.
The drug like everything else is manifesting through your own Mind.
How is Your Mind, this Matrix? Drugs are only a guide, You are Self
Realisation ~ Celebrations not Obsessions! No Abusing, don't flip,
burn-out, crash-out; with any 'come down', keep the clear harmonic.
Tuning naturally and Trust your inner Meditation to guide your light.

Shamans have been guiding us here into these fantastic worlds of Spirit but the Authorities have continuously demonized this activity. They obviously now don't speak for the Potential of this little, 'OM' 'Shiva' or 'Dr. Hoffman'. 'The Cosmic Serpent', by Jeremy Narby; and Carlos Casteneda, Ken Kesey, Fritjof Capra, and many more, have Courageously led us into these other Physics/Psychic/ Magic alternative 'dimensions'. Your Heart and Mind will reflect the drug like a mirror. It's certainly <u>Not</u> ready for everyone, especially when Governments continue their 'Inquisition' and Oppression of those who wish to go into these realms of discovery. To experience fully freely a Psyche*Odyssey, discovering where/who they are in this Cosmos and on this Natural Planet, in these sacred relationships. But these 'Controlling' forces continue their criminalised negativity, the repression, their Paranoia and help create these victims of the 'War on Drugs'. This Table is misleading, not giving a Real Sense; its amazing potential to go into/beyond your own Outer/Inner limits. But, says "a 'bad trip' can cause anxiety." What about a good trip? Can that be a catalyst and point you to your Divine Self-Realisation, to your Illumination and Liberation? There is more in this drop than they say or want you to know about, Mind-control and human power. Going Into the other realms of Tao, Synchronicity, Meditation, natural Transcendence of your Mind/Ego.This embraces and enhances your Cosmic reality and can take you to the stars * It can also lead some to doors of Addiction, Obsession, Fear and 'I' Craving Attachments, which is also the 'Human Condition'. Whether sex, drugs, rock and roll, or this Selfish Mind, being the Dominating Dictator, it depends on 'You'. You take Your Full Responsibility. You Open your own doors but do it Consciously, No Ego, Happily, Freely with the Full respect, confidence, grace and humble gratitude of a Shamanic ~ Spiritual quest; Not Coercive 'Conditioning' and Ego-Identification. Be Non-Attached, keep your Inner Prayer ~ Mantra in Your Clear, true heart; be equanimous. Know, let it go, flow with boundlessness.

	NAME	WHAT IS IT?	DEATHS in 2004
1	**Heroin**	From poppies grown mostly in Afghanistan	744
2	**Cocaine**	Made from coca shrubs from Colombia & Bolivia	147
3	**Barbiturates**	Synthetic lab-made drugs, used prominently in clubs	14
4	**Street Methadone**	Synthetic drug similar to heroin but less addictive	200
5	**Alcohol**	Brewed across the world in many different forms	22,000
6	**Ketamine**	Anesthetic drug popular on club & rave scene	N/A
7	**Benzodiazopines**	Tranquillizers used to beat anxiety & insomnia	206
8	**Amphetamines**	Synthetic stimulant snorted, mixed in drink or injected	33
9	**Tobacco**	Smoked. Most of the leaf comes from the Americas	114000
10	**Buprenorphine**	Opioid drug. Can be made in a laboratory	N/A
11	**Cannabis**	Plant. Easily cultivated in temperate climates	16
12	**Solvents**	Organic compounds found in glues, paints, lighter fluid	53
13	**4-MTA**	Amphetamine derivative	N/A
14	**LSD**	Hallucinogenic, synthetic drug more popular in 60s	N/A
15	**Methylphenidate**	Medicine, similar to amphetamines	N/A
16	**Anabolic Steroids**	Hormones used by body-builders and sportsmen	N/A
17.	**GHB**	Synthetic drug, sold as "liquid ecstasy"	3
18	**Ecstasy**	Synthetic drug in tablets; popular in dance scene	33
19	**Alkyl Nitrates**	Liquid, better known as "poppers"; inhaled	N/A

WHAT DOES IT DO?	UK Users
Sedative. Can be smoked or injected to produce a "rush" Users feel lethargic experience severe cravings for drug.	40,000
Stimulant. Increases alertness & confidence but raises heart rate & blood pressure, users will crave it.	800,000
Powerful sedatives. Widely prescribed as sleeping pills. Dangerous in overdose & now superseded by safer drugs.	Not many
Used to wean addicts off morphine & heroin because it is less sedating. Street versions may be contaminated.	20,000
Central nervous system depressant used to reduce inhibitions Higher doses lead to intoxication, coma & respiratory failure.	Most adults
Intravenous anesthetic used medically on human & animals. When taken in tablet form, it creates hallucinatory experiences.	Unknown
Most common prescription tranquilizers. Effective sedatives which have a calming effect, reducing anxiety, but are addictive.	160,000
Man-made drugs that increase heart rate & alertness. Users may feel paranoid. Newer form, methamphetamine, is very addictive.	650,000
Contains nicotine, a fast-acting stimulant highly addictive. Tobacco causes lung cancer & increases risk of heart disease.	12.5m
More expensive alternative to methadone used to wean addicts off heroin. Preferred by some addicts, can produce dependence.	Unknown
Leaves of cannabis sativa plant or resin can be smoked or eaten. A relaxant but stronger forms can also cause hallucinations & panic.	3m
Produces euphoria & loss of inhibitions similar to being drunk, but can cause blackouts & death.	37,000
Effects similar to ecstasy, & also known as "flatliners" Popular dance drug, resulting in feelings of euphoria.	Unknown
Man-made, has strong effect on perception. Effects include hallucinations & loss of sense of time. A "bad trip" can cause anxiety.	70,000
Chemical name for Ritalin, A stimulant drug used to treat children with attention deficit hyperactive disorder; helps them concentrate.	Unknown
Synthetic drugs having a similar effect to hormones such as testosterone. Can lead to liver, kidney and reproductive health problems.	38,000
The date rape drug, Gamma-hydroxybutyrate, is a sedative, relaxing effect, reducing inhibitions, can lead to stiff muscles and fits.	Not many
Causes adrenaline rushes & feelings of well-being, but also can cause anxiety & high body temperature.	800,000
Gives a strong, joyous rush & a burst of energy for a few minutes which quickly fades and can leave a powerful headache.	550,000

In August 2006, the Independent, London, published Professor Nutt's Drug table suggesting Alcohol and tobacco are more harmful than class A drugs, LSD and Ecstasy. This research was done by the House of Common's Science and Technology select committee. Politically It was disregarded by the Government. This farce continues until today, 2017, with Professor Nutt being fired in 2009 for his continued adherence to Scientific evidence. Now we have seen the legalization of marijuana in of all places, Washington state, Colorado etc. and California in January 2018, in the good old USA who were the principal Witchfinders along with their trusted lackey the UK. Government. Their anti-drugs policy was implemented throughout the world while at the same time it has been shown that the USA's, CIA were involved in massive smuggling operations of all drugs, principally Cocaine into the USA in order to buy weapons for their proxy, anti-government guerrilla groups, to destabilise countries that didn't toe the American, (for Democratic see Oligarchic) line! See also, 'Confessions of an Economic Hitman' by John Perkins, where he describes this covert economic warfare. The son of Pablo Escobar recently admitted that his father was working for the CIA! And throughout this period (over 50 years) ordinary people who want to get high are victimised on the scale of an Inquisition. This also applied to ill people who wanted to use marijuana to relieve their pain, eg. Multiple sclerosis and they were vehemently denied this humane right on the basis of Political expedience. This is disgusting and even though this situation has been aired in the subordinate media it has predominantly been demonized, marginalised and the people who are shining the light of truth on Conspiracies, as always have been ruined and imprisoned. WHY? Now medical marijuana/oil is legalized around the world/online from Canada to Australia. It's recently been allowed recreationally in Catalonia and today of all places Las Vegas, Nevada, USA! There is the realisation of an economic bonanza ready for harvesting and this cynically as usual is the main motivation for political change. Try and figure that out! Yet the UK still will not accept the reality of the scientific evidence so has continued the persecution of people for smoking weed

It is another sign of outrageous prosecution by despotic, plutocratic non-democratic, psychological warfare on people, and this class of dictator who are given the privilege, responsibility and power to serve 'people', are instead sociopathic, paranoid, egotistic, deranged, criminal maniacs and ignorantly motivated by personal profit. This is now obvious, and we should witness these real contradictions. We have to become conscious of a Orwellian matrix all around us! The hidden power of Conglomerates has to be exposed for the reinstatement of truth and our human Liberty. Since the 1960's with the Hippie and cultural, social, anti-war revolution, Governments continued to repress, oppress and brain-wash its people. This is an obvious and deliberate stance maintaining an elite status-quo economically and to expand an agenda of the NWO, Globalist, fascists. Imperialism, warmongering, insane inequalities are perpetuated again. There is information on every aspect of this brain-washing Matrix on the internet today. Crypto-Government-Corporate cabals are the ones who perpetrate and perpetuate these scenarios to maintain their Elite power! Just as in the time of Galileo who observed that the Earth, in fact orbited the Sun and not the other way round; the holy Pope made him 'recant' his scientific evidence for purposes of the church's religious power. It is no different today and we are still the victims. Prohibition one day and the next a miracle cure! Money and Power the bottom line. "There are more than 60,000 transnational corporations in the world. More than 50 of the largest one-hundred economies in the world are corporations. Transnational corporations hold ninety percent of all technology and product patents worldwide. Transnational corporations are involved in 70 percent of world trade. The top 737 of these super-corporations or 'super-entities' control 80% of the world economy. The top 147 super-corporations or 'super-entities' control 40% of the global economy through direct and indirect ownership or controlling interest. Hundreds of companies own the stocks and bonds of each other - they collectively own themselves. Hence, it becomes nearly impossible to trace the roots of ownership and control. From relative obscurity, they wield enormous control of national and global economies" Swiss Fed Institute Tech,2011

Healing (It) Sue Marvel
Vibration I can {feel} channel it ~
'Intention' is to be already healed.
Sending direct energy waves there ~
Sending a more Conscious frequency
Letting go of time ~ then you realise
It's fixed, defined, identified in your brain!
Then you let go ~ wet, as the falling rain,
dissolving ~ breath the source of all life.
Energy channeling ~ oxygen worker
Physical elements is our channel
without this sense, mind-body
we're fucked!
Surely that's not how
it's truly meant to be ~
Is anything meant to be?
Ask a lovely Lily

*

Awareness
"Fucked up ~
with Acid eyes!"
"Senility is wasted on most people"
Of course ~ it's not being Realised
(fearful ignorance) as a Creative force!
His life as Alternative Consciousness

*

Fire Dancer
Moon Force
effecting your live-blood stream ~
gravity, waters, senses, emotions.
'Energetic beings * Love Our Gaia'
(Not stuck in the Ego) his Immune system is so high!
Channeling, absorbing fully, Cosmic power ~

99% say "Yes"
Tapping into the Collective Un^Conscious?
Working on the Psyche from a true Heart ~
Connecting with that source of pure essence
Activates higher level perception ~ directing
higher energies to your higher Consciousness.
Trusting your Intuition, shit Yeah!
Free will, choice, natural rights of people, species
to decide, listening to that ~ or Fear Stops that!
Wanting to be happier everyday, clear blue sky.
A drug for Inspiration ~ however it works.
We're Humans and want to be ~ high!
Evaporating it ~ enjoying Perfection.
*Equality, beings * we're all unique…*
Whatever works for the greater good.
Respect for the laws of the Universe
*

Drawing
Intuition before ~
the logic Mind-sets
the flow of your gift.
Natural life force ~
flowing beingness
beyond the masks
*

Phaseic
Happy dripping
better to float
without it ~
In Tune
As It Is ~
Hey, it's non Stop!

Multitasking Waitress
Creative and superbly Inspiring.
Window into Conscious flowing ~
Entangled in Quantum Molecular
dimensions
*

You
"Your body is
Your Temple.
Depends who
You let into it"
Be Aware ~
*

What is the Point * Ultimately?
I never tapped
Into it…
an abstract being!
*A different * energy*
to be utilised ~ Uniquely.
A Creative, expressive
Loving Person
*

BaBa DaDa Style
Met at the Cabaret Qasar
I love Daliesque.
A surreal thread
thru a landscape
of Neon Giraffes
& the Intention ~
of exquisite Love.
*Multi*dimensions*
Centre of relaxation

Got Any Obstacles
Mind communicating
"You Can't Paint!"
Breaking through Fear, ZAP!
Demons Inside You ~ letting
Abstract creations of energy
be expressions of what is real.
*

Cocoon Focusing on/in It
A true artist or fake egoist ~
Driving that Bus - Not Stopping!
Who are we to Judge any one?
Uniquely being in Tune
A natural ~ that's the pure essence
focusing on remaining in the Present.
Enjoying life, in Lake 'Ch
with Mum and Dad, Family, Friends,
Pachamama, Planet Earth, Cosmos
*

We all Know the Truth
Only have to remind Ourselves ~
Our energetic channel Is ~ forever Changing
Intention, using that higher frequency
to support Healing Mother Earth.
Using that flow of Consciousness.
More and more Crystalline atoms nurturing us.
Keep working with structures in a Space lattice.
Product of the environment, "I Love you ~
A delicate gaze with such inner beauty.
Mixing within Oceans of Compassion

being
In It
Feeling ~ Feeling
Why not - Why Not?
Amazing inner Magic
of the Loving heart
*

Maori Taonga
Letting go of my style
Singing from the Heart
lights went on all over ~
Using those channels
Against domination
I think that's elemental Soul.
Driving with the Gypsy Kings
*

Spiral Images
Acknowledging, those emotions presented.
Abstract is Spiritual ~ Objects manifesting in 3D
Watching a Rajasthani painter paint a perfect
miniature picture of a King or God; realism's scenario.
The detail was so Incredible that you could Not deny,
that this Is the true, Physical likeness of a King or God!
I like Abstract Expressionism ~ Collective Unconscious
beyond any material concept of what Kingship or God is.
I feel this is more in tune, essence, flowing with the infinite.
In Visible ~ Inter dimensional, honey moon, sea breezes, free.
Sharing that energy, light Love there is no absolute definition.
Time and Time again ~ being open, in Tune to the boundless.
It all comes back to the same thing of physical transcendence.
Or we make Icons, Idols of those who want to rule our Minds.
And our Universal Spirits ~ become slaves, a Matrix definition
to serve a superior, despot King; be dominated or have liberty

Smart Soulbot

"Having a Religion or not Is ~ I know what I like; to be free"
You must have something ~ to connect to the Universe.
You take your Peace with you inside, wherever you go.
Incantations ~ exorcise your Mesmer Conditioned eyes.
Awesome on the block, that's what no rules do for you.
Hypocrisy, democracy, no he's just a hick from Alberta.
Psychology of the VIP room; hey Bill fuck off!
Auto rotation ~ slowly slowly slowly…
falling faster faster * heart's in your mouth.
Even the dogs loved it, tails all wagging ~
doesn't chase, walks back, stops running,
to reboot his trees

*

Transing Responsibility

Losses, letting go ~ to trusting in that Spirit.
"Are You American, have you been in Jail?"
I want to follow the Sun, in a Happy Circle.
To feel at Peace, being in my Space
"I need to move out of this Studio!"
Put it all together on an Isolated beach.
"Amazing not * being off my head!"
Tranced Universo Parallelo Party.
Dancing with the celestial flow ~
Linked to the Modern day ~
Tribal hippie Cosmic Yin*Yang.
I Choose to be in the positive
Embrace all (the Godly bits)
Embrace all the Good bits!
Leading by example ~
Who would Choose
to be Miserable
and not to See?
The Beauty of Life

Revelations of Nisagadatta's chai wallah
Always on the trail of Perfect, Divine, dhamma law.
Then, this and that Karma, blossoms over time ~
"Physical is Temporal, no past or future exists
Invisible is the Eternal"

*

100000000000000))))))))))))))))%
Darwin never experienced the Spiritual World
of the Cosmic Serpent, he recanted his findings.
At the end, 'Origin Of Species' was a limited edition.
The Mind is So, so beautiful ~ Narsisstic to Itself only.
Got to tell the Mind to shut up, there's more to life. But
Mind won't tell you that. "Don't use Programming words"
You have to give up everything, all thoughts.
Is this limited Mind going to speak for us?
Because now I got to be free and move into
Awareness of New Dimensional paradigms.
Awareness speaks for itself
Not letting Master Mind mass control us, as it wants.
"Is it better landing on the Moon or Understanding
the Nature of the finite Mind-set; of all things, infinitely?"
To see the light you have to Meditate, sit still under a tree.
Quietly, calming the Mind to observe you, witnessing itself.
Not the I think dimension, go into; 'I am knowing now dimension

*

Super Mad Beauty
Darling ~ Selfishly.
You taught me how,
to go out of my Mind!
Full Power Wizardry
within floral, fractal ~
dimensions of nature

> My dreams Alive <
"We deserve to have an Abundance
And to Share it for the Greater good.
Open to receive now goes round in a cycle.
If you don't think you deserve it
You'll never bloody get it!"
True conspiracies of a fluoride load of paste,
he's walking through the mist with bad boys.
*

Healthy Peaks - Full Whiteys!
London's bloody hard and heavy! Classy Predators.
Left for the Brighter light ~ Out for the natural Good.
Centering as a Shield ~ 'Go to Goa to recharge your soul'
Global beings chilling out in the Sun with hippie Intentions.
Rainbows of Interplanes ~ flows, glows, human membranes.
Open, realigning, the base charka to Ancient India's energy.
Being stuck into Survival ~ tapping into Spiritual Abundance!
Why be Miserable? Make a BIG HAPPY poster!
Get a suit in Delhi, good for convincing people!
High frequencies ~ beautiful light, I love it Bright.
What's that mean though in Reality, where is that?
Alters in the process ~ DNA; formulating New Ideas.
*SYNCHRONOUS * DIMENSIONS * PERPETUALLY*
*

A Job, Debts, Remortgage, S/he's pinned down!
Run for your Life ~ ditch it all and survive.
"Happy, You have to go Up!"
Slave, You wanted to fly...
Fine Tuning a croaking frog.
*Fine Tuning * Acacia DMT.*
Out in the middle
of nowhere

Girlfriend Sharing

"Depends what drug you're on or not!"
Is there any low feeder who will rip you off?
Free Free ~ no Scare, no paranoia; honour.
"Sometimes people only listen to the drugs &
the drugs say "take more." Need to be Aware.
Centering LSD *~* energy from Inside out
Realise > No Addiction & No Obsessions.
Cosmic Feeling * Cosmic Healing
*

Perfect Natural Magic

Open Psychic Channel ~ can be Uplifting, transcending it all...
Cy Twombly's Connection >:< Quattro Stagione, Purest abstractions.
Feeling fresh, light, Prima Vera's delicate chiaroscuro, Cosmic balance.
*

Laughing and Touching

Mall Robbers playing a bad Santa...
Look out for a man carrying a bucket.
What to do? What a complete asshole!
It's against the law to Not help people
coming down from the Barrio ~
Making love or killing, in the City of God?
These Actors are Real People...
A True Fairy tale in a high max security, real bad Jail.
And those secured in middle, Upper class ghettoes?
Rearranging the teacher's words, being good parents.
What about the biological warfare of vaccines and Flu?
*

Robot Fucker

Good but not good enough ~ Identities that never met.
What you take is your business. Defeat, Repeat, Incomplete.
Man Made ~ MDMA; Organic spores of bliss.
Highlighting the cloudless Sky over a lagoon.
Timeless dreaminess in your Spiritual kiss

Love
Falling
Takes time ~
Of course, I have
Feelings ~
Think of Today…
Wanting to Change it
Do You Trust me?
I have no choice but to…
You're the most honest person I ever met.
Taking it as Shanti as a dolphin ~
as Peaceful as can be
*

Unimaginable
flying in Anjuna ~
genie out of the bottle
Hoffman was good, to them.
"Turn on *Tune in* Drop out * Become aware"
Out of the Mind-sets ~ peddling, Insanely happy
*

Greed Can Not be the Goal
Making it as easy as possible.
Drop the outline ~ being free,
do you want to make…
Money or want to have FUN;
are they Mutually-Exclusive?
Dancing with the devil ~
Caught in that moment
*

I Smart
Nothing Wrong
in Learning how
to play the game is there?
Goa: 'Happier here than anywhere else'

Enforcing the Human Rights of Girls

*'Bride kidnapping, also known as marriage by abduction or marriage by
capture, is a practice in which a man abducts the woman he wishes
to marry. Bride kidnapping has been practiced around the world and
throughout history. It continues to occur in countries in Central Asia,
Caucasus region, and parts of Africa, and among peoples as diverse
as the Hmong in Southeast Asia, the Tzeltal in Mexico, Despite its
illegality, in many primarily rural areas, bride kidnapping, known as ala
kachuu (to take and flee), is an accepted, common way of taking a wife.
Approximately half of all Kyrgyz marriages include bride kidnapping, of
those kidnappings, two thirds are non-consensual. Research by NGO's
give estimates from a low of 40% to between 68 and 75 percent of all
marriages in Kyrgyzstan involved bride kidnapping'.   Wikipedia.*

*

First Free Generation ~ Liberated Women

*Dreams finally came true with you; naked in a meadow by Moscow.
One look ~ so romantic; the World can now be their Oyster, a new view.
"I fully corrupted these girls, they're corruptible", the Cossack said.
Maui to Yellowknife, being in Love, perfect, if I'd met any other woman.
Cosmic exploration of the Heart, to the end, then comes the ending,
the end the end end end end end end end end end end end, changes ~
Showing the Mountain no respect; beautiful energy, with or without her.
As long as its Full Power * Full Energy * Full Feeling
No separation, no duality ~ together in endlessness.*

*

In Absolute

*Each Moment Is Present, without any thinking ~
Ubiquitous * Enlightenment > only an Overloaded Word.
Relativity of Perfect*ion is Perfect, each instant here now.
Don't need to rationalise about it, no need; Wanting Forever.
No identifying, judging; Realisation can be as it is * nothingness.
Silence Is still Golden not a forked tongue!*

<u>Dead Pan ~ American Gods Gone Up in Toxic Smoke</u>
They say the Internet was Invented by the Porn Industry!
It's not Chillums it's the *LSD* > Man in a Cosmic cloak.
Mirror opposites ~ going into symbiotic, kaleidoscopes.
The Sistine Chapel in black, no judgments, relent, intent.
Apocalypse Now, be clear of all the habits & addictions!
"Likes waking up to the smell of Napalm in the morning"
*

<u>Freaky Key</u>
Every moment ~ Is Important
Got to Keep remembering that.
Or not, just living that, happiness.
From everything ~ All is a Reflection
No Limiting ~ beyond any system, our Mind-sets!
Sent interstella strawberries from another galaxy and
Magical Mushroom spores, existing Inner * Outer Space.
Helping our Minds to survive, crossing the Egoist Matrix.
So use them to say *__Hallo__* in Alien*able Communication.
Going through the boundaries ~ Fuck it, accept it, deal with it.
Live in the garden, "every time I have less, I feel I have more"
Very nice things, the Things are Owning them, they really do ~
Scheme > desperate, hope, going through Mental, 'Imaginary'
loss that seems Real, very Real, it always feels so Real to me!
Reality, upside down disillusions; what's that mean ~ changing
*

<u>Keep it simple continuum</u>
'Try to be an Angel to someone'. Who you calling a barbarian?
Instinctive, Free from Thinking-Ego, like an irrational Neanderthal.
Thought-Mind Identity into the body only relates to Things or not.
You paint your own picture through Consciousness; Start, Finish.
Life is timeless Singularity * reflections of conceptual Relativity...
The canvas is blank, just flowing throughout the whole.
'Through the Finite, the Infinite is reflected ~
"I want someone I can go out and play with"

Rio Negro*Lighthouse

"Humans are the dreaming of Dolphins ~
Turn it down! New Ideas, fantasies, visions.
"I can't see me ~ going to Rishi Kesh Babaji"
I'm just happy sitting here, gazing at the sea.
Temptation changes with innocent children ~
Protect our most naturally, priceless resource.
Terra-forming, already growing piglets in Korea;
in this Green house, a carbon dioxide Scarecrow!
Unhappy because he's not well connected to Earth.
Every animal and chemical has a role to play, It's Vital!
"Encountering a Blue Whale off the bow of my Kayak."
Tenderness of an Elephant, magic of salmon migration.
Blood of everything in Flora ~ Ownership is Stewardship!
'A plant is everyone's, how can you put a fence around it?'
They clear-cut mountains, killing ancient, sacred, Spirit trees!
Ignorance of greedy Exploitation, is that any excuse today?
Criminals burning it in the fields while everyone's sleeping

*

Mother Load

Peaking In Tune to Shiva's Moon.
"The dancin' got me into the trance"
Gave him everything he wanted ~
Laughing Cosmic, I understand but I
don't know! Investing in a bottle of drops.
Power of auto-suggestion, 30 secs. rushes!
Self-introspection, not a parasite in Paradise.
Still a hippie ~ "I'm dancing for Mother Earth!"
"Can or can't make the connections anymore.
The Universe provides what you really need
If you allow it to....

<u>All Bi Polars</u>
'Dreaming the dream of the dream dreaming'
Psychosis from Society
Running around for Me
Higher frequency ~
Incarnated E.T.
White powders
*

<u>Beautiful</u>
If they survive in Nepal, got a good Immune system!
Is there any difference between Ambition & Dream?
Feel like I'm home
Astral ~ feeling
Freedom of Spirit
Lucky Karma ~ lovely dhamma
In a summer's wildflower meadow.
*

<u>Gokharna</u>
A holiday from Goa ~
"If I was organised I'd be dangerous!"
'Mother's Day'
"I Love being a Woman
*Fun * Finding my Power."*
@MySuperGoddess.net
*

<u>Grass roots tribal</u>
"Let the Relationship grow…
Relate in the moment ~ relating
not a Relationship."
Trust and it's Always new… this reflection.
Russian girls are so alive, now (they were so repressed).
Indian children come running to you happy and (unstressed)
excited, still Pure Innocence; unprogrammed in a War zone!
Thank you for reminding me again, 'that Love always changes'

Blessing
There's no following ~
listen to, transmute your vibration
Being ~ Truthful to Yourself.
"I have to let you go, it will break my heart!"
Caught in Illusions of Pain, on an Insane plane.
Let it go ~ into natural flow
Completely Trust in the Trust trusting
not the desirous, lustrous golden dust
sparkling in your shaved, pulsating star.
*
Just don't get caught
Secret ~ Ice Cream eater…
Have to express it ~ vibrations of 'your' Chakras.
Santa Fay ~ you begged me, 'for us' to stay, together.
Bitter not better, why? Lots and lots of Mind-feeling Sets.
Using your Imagination, through the end of Time and Space.
Finding Yourself through a projected Image, in a nursery rhyme.
Language of waves ~ not accepting people been treated as slaves.
RELATIONSHIP giving, allowing as much freedom as possible.
Reflecting Myself in You ~ Destiny is True.
Ignoring It or not being Aware of it, changing.
Synchronicity of the ~ moment to moment.
*Love Yourself * Open Your heart*
Whatever energy is up, Perfect as it is.
Task, is to surrender to life, to what is…
We have to flower ~ to bloom, no gloom.
Could you move please, you're standing
in front of the Sun; Apollo is here to transform its radiance ~
"How to deal with the energy and make a blessing out of it?"
Let it flow, no stopping Crown Chakra's white light, beaming
*In a luscious Lily pod * All Opening * sweet monsoons in Goa*

Eden Kits in the Pink, Orange Tulip
Just being in this Paradisiacal garden ~
Just being in the middle of the ego-game.
Programmed # IIIIIII 'MINDSETS'
Power bodies, Positive vibes, into the Wilderness ~
Imitating the Valkyries, full respect for strong workers.
Golden smiles in her full length, Bora Bora, naked pareu.
Her coloured tattoos full trancing, on the dance floor ~
Psychedelic energy exciting hot chemicals in her nexus.
Feeling the music inside, with her hot body not her brains.
"The Oneness of LSD; embracing ~ Super Aware of Chi"
Seeing into her throbbing, Venus' veins
swimming in her molten, lava streams,
gliding through her eyes' light beams ~
Reconnected, it was so beautiful
Trans formed ~Trance sensed.
To Manifest in multi*dimensions
Energies to balance In and out ~
helping to lift it up, helping to light up
all the frequencies spinning in Vortices.
Transitional sacred vibes of Rainbow holograms
getting closer to invisible energy, Galaxy of devotion.
We cannot Stop the Ocean, extend or enhance nature.
Embracing full reflections ~ because You have it inside You.
Find Yourself in Love ~ Nothing else.
Cosmic expansion no more duality.
You are the Ultimate * Happiness
*

His Nature
She's a Witch
Burn her Alive!
"I'm from the future!"
Full Passionate lights
"I want your nectar!"

Gamboges' Profundity
Sun Holograms create different projections ~
Top Predator Heart (blood), Healing Shamans' (DMT.).
Ayuhuascan gifts > Parallel Worlds of < Universal Atoms.
*Crystals shimmering on Atlantis * women spinning in the spring.*
Took me by the hand, renaissance in tune with her light, pink moon
Me, I cross worlds, you too?
*
Cool Synergy
No more Duality ~
Only Peace, Happy Love
Real Power <:> ALL ONE
Natraj dancing in Parvati's energies
*on a Shiva*Shakti, rainbow aura bridge.*
Unity within a divine vision ~ spectrum
Diversity, transcending beating Hearts,
black holes, exploding shooting stars!
Into the eclipse of a Microcosmic Sun.
Inspiration, expiration ~ the navel axis.
Creative energies of the Pranasphere
*Prima Star * Sushima's Spiral column.*
Force of Life ~ rising, sharing vibrations
Completely Pure the frequency of death.
Can't kill them ~ Immortals, their full freedom.
Going through transformation can be confusion ~
Not the Circus, so let it be ~ every moment, Lovely.
*Prana is the key to supra-astral multi*dimensionality.*
Giving energy out each moment, Kundalini rising up.
We are frequency ~ every moment a new beginning.
Life's Vibrations rising to an apex, out of body sensations.
Lotus position

Immortality Force
"Shiva is a Concentration"
to dissolution of ~ 'Self's Creation'
Atomiques Bombes de l'Amour
Explosions of Love ~ Power of Life
*

'Rain is liquid Sunshine'
Letting things flow ~ through us
Vibrating of a woman is different to a man.
Cells concentrated in 3 dimensional density.
In tune with the Moon ~ Heart frequency
The One I came to Love
You see astral space in their eyes of Innocence.
*

Prima Dolce Vita Principality
Not allowed to Enjoy yourself,
gathering in large Numberos!
Consciousness wherever you are…
You're at the right place at the right time ~
It's all Timing, You're Creating ~ Your Own Reality.
Your will choosing how to respond, painfully or not?
Everything is there, the cause, taking your attention.
*

Alien * Off Planet
Death-finition, give it to a rat once a month!
DNA. just went off grid, Target unidentified…
No Soul, No Humanity, No Empathy, Heartless.
De programme, Defrag, memory wiped clean, rebooted.
"You have to stand up for your rights or you don't have any"
Iranian lips sucking up and down my bell end!
A Khmer with knives, she was fuckin' lethal!
He was a Hell's Angel then discovered Ecstasy.
It's just another perception, way of thinking.
We're all dancing for Mother Earth

My favourite woman is Venus on the terrazzo
What's a definition of Collaboration? Natural energetic particles.
Channeling the Creative-Art, Channeling Thoughts-Mind-sets...
Channeling Life-force, Channeling No copyrights, free expression.
"I don't do dramas anymore" because it's only particles processing.
It's no Mind, no Ego, no anything, existing infinite Space
Processes always changing, detached, from any subject.
Cause and effect, action-reaction is karmic (if you want).
"I take care of Dhamma ~ Dhamma takes care of me"
With those seeds of ignorance, fear, anxiety, selfishness!
Leads to not getting caught in the ego habit of Identification.
*Extra sensorial * Galaxies within Galaxies, what to do man?*
Bio-Cosmic fields you call my emotions, desires, ambitions,
darling; reflection of your truest conscious in deep stillness.
I can't give the commitment you want to permanent unreality.
*On a roll, no soul ~ leads to liberation * Maximum light*
*

Blinking Sputnik 1
UFO. ½ ecstasy, ½ mescaline, energetic fruit salads.
No Ego, No Mind just a process of Inspirational change.
The river changes, the body changes the Mind changes,
electricity giving us the BIG illusion of some unity, entity!
FREEWHEELING beyond any 'Technique', thank you ~
so no body, no death, no fear and terror, nothing to lose ~
*SUPER FAST PROCESSES * faster than your Mind's eye.*
*

VALIUM Fascination
What, to calm your mind down…
Meditation, allurement; be who you are.
Concentrate on that, it's real, the breath.
But I'm even unaware of my breathing!
Having some gratitude ~ Being here now.
It's not the addiction it's the Temptation!
"One cannot live by drugs alone"

<u>*Spreading the Love*</u>
"I wish they'd nuke them; the Koreans, I really do!"
No one in their right mind would do it but these just
want to cause trouble." What's the new capital of Israel?
"What can you do about it? Nothing! It's just commercial!"
Women skied one side, men the other.

*

<u>*Warhol:*</u> *I like the abstract rather than any 'Realism images'.*
Shadow represents nothingness; cropped, so no reference
to its Object {beingness} with Cosmic diamond dust giving
*Light effects * reflections of the Source (Celestial stars).*
Looking - to make - a Good Deal; is Life not all in vain?
Whatever you Feel is Real, who needs an Ego's Brain?
Stretching it to the Outer Limits, before the next War!
"I am that I am" ~ the rain that I feel, that feeds Life.

*

<u>*Dominating Captain Zircon*</u>
Once You interpret it, You're back in the 'I Smart Program'.
"How do you know?" "The Programs, drive our fears dear!"
Born from the Cosmos, it will give you what you need to live.
Ma India slowly gets to you; Spiritually, Wisdom is Wisdom ~
Living myths beyond words, naturally, pilgrimage to a Temple.
3500 year old mango tree, growing in a 2 billion year old Valley.
Amazing Nature Programming, whatever makes it up ~ flowing
'Man drives the Machine' Control & Controlling ~ Perpetually
Emotional! Life taking care of us being here **free feelings.***
"Women fetch the food, Men are the sleeping member!"
You already know it ~ breath, gone into the far galaxies.
All about dropping, letting go (Concepts of a Mind-Set).
Only way to be ~ a bit of Kosmique, travelling, Anarchie.
Putting fragrant flowers and young coconuts into the river.
Chanting ~ "I'll go anywhere for someone who Loves me"

Govinda's Singing
Nothing better than the Monkey brain ~ they have feelings too!
Let it run itself, Control is another opposite of Free Love.
You're looking at someone who's telling you ~
that they don't want to be with you Anymore!
"Carry your Ashram in your heart ~
You only have to
Shine"
*

A Perfect Moment
It could be ~
the Rainbows
in the Sky
It's all Divine
Consciousness
*

Morphing Auras
Sampling ~ Balance of the 5 elements…
*Earth *Air *Fire* Water ~ Celestial Space*
And Italian babas dancing on the ethereal plane.
A Great Catalyst, Cosmic Fractals; It's all truly Divine ~
We don't even exist as you think ~ it's not even real, time is not mine.
When we fly, immersed in the light * when we open into infinite night.
Shining all around * Lovely Smiles, feeling connected to the Cosmic
energies energies energies energies energies energies energies
energies energies energies energies energies energies energies
energies energies energies energies *energies energies* ***energies***
energies ***energies*** *energies energies energies energies* ***energies***
energies *energies* ***energies*** *energies* ***energies*** *energies energies*
energies energies ***energies*** *energies energies* ***energies*** *energies*
energies *energies energies* ***energies*** *energies energies* ***energies***
energies energies energies energies energies energies
energies energies energies energies energies energies

<u>Perfect Illusion Verite</u>
"We have to see we are acting; a Nouveau vague cinema"
Illuminated process ~ closer to the Galaxy, beyond density.
We're lucky sufferers * accepting the Ultimate, if we know it ~
frequencies arising, falling, arising, frequencies falling, arising
Impermanent light to light Inspiration, No self, Ego, 'Me' thee,
here's just flow ~ no need of the suffering of Identifying with it.
More Consciousness ~ all healing, no need of placebos.
¼ hits, opening (separate) doors & windows to Surreality.
250 exponential microns, mushrooming to the Power 10'.
Depends on the Crystals * keeping True Energetic Synergy.
Tantra fusion's Timelessness, My 'No Time' Space is precious.
Shiva ~ is beyond Yoga, beyond Meditation, beyond the Moon.
Two energies that are one ~ Celestial river born
*

<u>Dancing-Dead Troops</u>
Who's controlling Your Mind
Your Thinking?
Find a compromise, make an agreement.
"She was my cell mate"
*

<u>Junkie on Freak Street</u>
"I'll sleep when I'm dead"
No Recognition ~ the Seed of all seeds.
'Cannot put Love in a Cage'
No attachment, Pure heart and Nothing back.
"She's in that Zone, inside a Pure, smile moment"
"Innocent, natural, smile or the Mind, Spangled Baba?"
A couple making Love ~ being United or Separated.
Receiving all the Love ~ Giving of the Universal heart.
"They're not Contaminated like us"; open, native people.
You'll be amazed, when I saw the Invisible energy field.
Turning into Angels * In front of my eyes.
Reincarnation * rebirthing of Love * light

Beautiful life in India
'Lucy in the Sky with Diamonds'.
"No such thing as Bad drugs dude, but Bad Brain…
For your Blame game, a Jackass from the beginning!"
The War on drugs! Smoking King, le Baba's magic potion ~
"Take LSD, sell everything and come to India." Co creation,
*Procreation, Permeation, Correlation * Saraswati's darshan…*
"just because you got Democracy doesn't mean you got freedom"
*

Basic Nature
Prefer to be an Alpha,
to mate with an Alpha.
The Best genes ~
the leader of the Pack.
Strongest or Brightest.
King Arthur who, Merlin?
"Is it possible for a hippie from the Cosmodrome to hook
up with a beautiful Astrophysicist from Mission Control?"
"There's some pretty shallow Astrophysicists out there!"
*

Solipsistic Fire Juggling
'The bad, bad seed' as seen Incessantly on TV!
I didn't see that one coming, right in the back!
"Give me those flip flops!" or I will kill you!
Are you ever hearing what you're saying?
Living in a Rose teepee, gleaming inside you and me.
Decadence, perversion, corruption of Western culture.
Can't stand it anymore ~ a pointer, to drop out, Now.
You're taking the piss; use me, don't abuse me dear!
You really don't know any better, what a shame.
Who and how ~ could you betray such a Love?
Consciously, realizing the delusional mind.
Forgiveness is empathy from the heart

Sufi Test > of an Existential Goth!
"As soon as you're old enough to drink,You can drive!"
Met Jim Thompson's friend in the Kali Bar!
"Nothing is True, Everything is Permitted"
Hasan al Sabbah ~ found A Savage Night…
"Amongst a Red Harvest, with a Serial Killing Priest.
What could be a better plot?" You can't make it up!
"My ex-father in law is a mystic yogi,
works for the Post Office"
*

Hanging In Tehran > Shock, Awe, Horror, Terror!
Ok, I deserved it? "You have my head but not my faith"
'Made many Christians by burning them with Kerosene'
"In-Tolerance everybody's releasing from their Karma!"
Ok, I desired it; fell on an Emperor's Peacock throne ~
Reactions from the past, going to come back to haunt me!
From Saturn's green reapers, making the Rules with
ignorant, painful vengeance, until Transcendence…
"The wise don't lament for the alive or dead"
Dropped the Obsidian swords ~
female frequency
*

Divine Starburst
"The Illusion is Real, It's just we Identify with it"
Causing reaction, causing reaction until we break
the chain ~ Atomic, galactic, central fusion, energy.
"Don't leave home without one"
The eight directions of a pedigree, Party Yogi.
Sees right through it, Soul Food, "being who I am"
That other sweet Heart who went to Heaven through you.
Found it existing in the body and Mind ~ changing Images
to a Good Guy, keeping the bombs out of y/our backyard.
Told when to Jump, all the strong cells survived the weak.

They Run the Matrix
She sees it ~ Exactly for what it is…
He knows what's happening in a War!
"To keep a bunch of Jackasses with MI6's in Line!"
"Imposing Order in the World and Kill all the People
who don't tow the Line." Sheep need to be put to sleep ~
They have no Idea of Compromise; If you didn't have to-
Fighting a War, Mad, got balls of Male testosterone ~
Sitting around doing Nothing, nurturing a parasite,
hatred with a Religious Zealism put on top of it.
Winding everyone up ~ Like a bunch of Toys!
Phosphor bombed, took their vital Resources.
Outspent them on the Biggest, deadliest Gun!
Of course it's Fuckin Horrible!"
*

Don't buy into any of those lines
"Don't think of it as Snow, see it as crystal Sunshine"
'Welcome to the Failing Catamites of Miserland'
The hummings and hawings; "Do Not Pass Go!"
"There's No Money in the Cure" -'Medical Industry'
"Conforming Stereotypes of blackest tyranny, history,
you're America you got all the money in the World!"
"Rather put a bullet in their head, than give them Ketamine!'
150gms; 85%, $5 grams of speed, scourge! And six days
weaving in a tinfoil hat as the Government's shooting EMF.
beams at you. Crystal Meth, Speed, Acid together, spangled!
'A nice Psychedelic culture' my Psycho-activated friend!
*"Living in **Transcendence** ~ Observing the Holy Grail"*
"All it is: Is only a drug, the rest is a lie. Ask a Shaman.
Consciously; why give so much Power to Drugs?"
Experience, a Catalyst for you ~ Intensifies

Thinking Is Too Much Mind ~ Be Kind
'But we got a Brain to train' (beyond insane).
Told don't acknowledge it only physicality!
Of course no ambition, society's definition.
It's better defeating the Will Power, why?
Surrendering to the beach time sunshine.
Is it so Important what You, really Think?
Now I know, you're an Alien, showing more empathy and
Positive energy flow than our elected, sociopath leaders.
Coke killed the culture + Meth amphetamine showed up!
How to let go, how to do that purring like your pussy cat,
tuning in at different levels, enjoying Cosmic meanings?
Playing with the nucleus of your beautiful Lover's heart.
Shamans in touch with Orchids, Charas, fresh Marijuana.
Before the 'drugs of the axis of evil', they were Medicine.
Help psychotics with LSD & ecstasy come to their senses.
Sub-atomic levels of Vibration, DNA, MDMA, letting it go ~
Protection of Lovers, hippies, free thinkers, poets, travellers.
Our Spiritual healers bringing ~ gifts of Consciousness
*
You build your dreams
Reality of Illusions ~ Timeless essence.
Her Mons Veneris playing in my Milky Way.
"What's in any wo/man's head, heart?"
"I'm a human not a precious Jewel"
Lost in the Mind-Forms-Paradigm.
Only thinking about the Objectives
not inner Space of Consciousness.
*WHICH ART THOU HERE * NOW*
The pure and simple natural reality
*'CONCEPTUAL * REALISATION'*
You have been conditioned mate…
Duality to recognise the Singularity.
Who I Am for Real

No ~ Coincidentals

"Drugs and Imprisonment in US; the perfect way
to Control People" (As well as everything else!)
"Give them what they want", bet my life on it.
Staying on a Reservation; giving them just
enough to kill themselves. "TB. Blankets for
your Teepee?" No Sociopathic self respect!
Stage manage Capitalism, Free Competition.
Government monopoly, Kontrols them all.
Creates a Gap for negativity and greed,
jealousy, egoism, racism, separation.
'Psychology' for coercing our society,
give it out ~ Getting more Authority!
Delusional, making them believe in it.
Having no Control! No Empowerment ~
Take your daily, double dose of Vicaden.
Get rid of your depression, try a Happy Pill.
Addicted by a white man, in a white suit!

*

The Blue Pill

"Guess what I got ~
A New dealer - doctor.
Selling Zoloff - go to sleep.
It'll be fine in the morning…
Get me out because all the points and centre sucks!
Narrow - minded, stuck to your Identity in-fidelity.
Craving, Addiction, No ambition, Obsessional!
ADHD. for what? My energy is focused on
being as Free ~ Objective as One can be.
Life-force frequency, lose your unconscious
ego ~ with whatever. "Thank-god it's Friday!"
"I'm an environmental Activist, who are You?"
"Not in the package I expected; natural in her own way"

<u>More Macho, Got to use that stuff!</u>
"The thing is to Start... And I'll take the trophy!
All women can't be passive; looks like I Like you ~
not to whore herself out. "Who wants a line of coke?"
Whatever, you can have a good time, but
I can't sell myself, for the fun of the game.
He's married with kids and won the Prize...
She's always fuckin' with me ~ that's fair.
"I hope you get mauled by a f..... Bear!"
I took everything of hers to the dump.
He's a paddler with a stick of dynamite!
'ACT ~ Alternative Crime Terrorist'.
Wicked night in a forgotten blues bar...
golden sequined lesbians fell from a star.
Red lights of hot, lascivious love's desire.
*

<u>Do they let Babas into Tibet?</u>
"Letter from our Ashram allowed us into Stonehenge!"
The Deep state, they want to break it for the future.
For them it's a horrible full Moon without a profit!
Raring to go ~ Freed it all up, consciously.
"Life is beauty full, hey!" She's full Angel.
Super model of fairies, just hanging loose ~
Meditation is a lovely balance of mind Space
to everything else ~ letting go, being detached.
*

<u>Fortien Belt</u>
Vasco de Gamma rays * waltzing with Dukkha and Sukkha.
Through a Pigeon hole, you see, she's been fuckin' a robot!
'Patriotism' 'Private Property', words giving us Chronic pain.
Add in Capitalism, Fundamentalism, Holy Religion, Oligarchy.
War, Corruption, Dividing and Conquering, Imperialist, Invasion.
When Mind is Ultra-Pure, for some and not for others ~ rolling.

<u>Non-Interested Mental Movement</u>
Everything lives in the Present ...
Yoni masseuse, the grace to impart.
Healing just coming through me....
Not looking, the undoing, the being.
Karma knots, concepts blocking energy.
Expect Nothing, everything is good and
enjoy the unforeseen, around the corner ~
*

<u>Insanely Happy Vortex</u>
Stimulation, simulation, needless needles!
Lost Yourself to addiction, its temptation, attracted by its grip!
Little choice, Powerlessness ~ "I gave up everything!"
Exploits you, doesn't want to have any sense of You!
Being Oppressed by the system, Mind; see through it.
Finally Surrendering to my true, Cosmic self.
Falling into consciousness ~ Initiating
something Amazing has happened…
The thoughts you put out on the ethereal
with the Merkaba kid, spinning his way to Venus.
Two counteractive fields ~ whirling in the same Space.
Spiritual Grace
*

<u>'The more you steal the butter!'</u>
They shoot deserters don't they but not the usurious Bangsters?
'Our systems have detected unusual traffic from your network…
we are checking if this is really you sending requests or a Robot'
Methadone, wall to wall junkies, "I wanna taste her oil"
"They know if you're not from Russia, when you smile"
If you're happy you are making other people happy.
*Everything from the heart not mind * Is Spiritual Life.*
"Yeah some mad stuff went on"

Holocaust deprogramming
Lack of talent endangers Japan's Porn Industry.
He shit through the eye of a needle onto her face!
People are designed to believe their programming.
Insulted, we can't do anything about it... Ignore it!
You gotta have a bit of pain to sing the blues
don't you think?
*

Long before we invented fire
Law of nature ~ 'where there is sweetness there are ants'
This Program called Earth, symbiosis, actually is creating us ~
Why should you be happy, don't you feel guilty, any remorse?
Unaware, "I could breathe, fresh Cosmic oxygen" Life force...
Psycho Active, Trance Central, rising up like a fiery Phoenix!
Being surrounded by people who didn't resonate with me.
A crazy-mad chef, I have to hold my breath and anger.
"Sir, permission to speak freely?" "I need a holiday!"
Underwater Goggles, went to Moscow by the sea.
Sputniks shooting straight up through the sky.
*

Gives me the willies
Nobody really can know the past or future only the here and now ~
They were selling people for over 200 years, it makes an imprint, mum.
Happy, there's no bombs going off or people coming around to kill 'em!
All my life I've tried to stay away from the troubles...
Being proper fucked up is a good feeling sometimes.
The Mind just can't conceive of something FORMLESS
Eternal Space is NOTHINGNESS as there is No Object
to fill in the gaps between 'My' thoughts with 'Mine' Thing.
Realising that Universal Intelligence is in each of our cells.
The Subject is beyond the Ego's self-seeking Mind-Objective.
There is nothing to hold onto, no 'Me', possession, attachment.
You are flowing in the stream of Consciousness which is truly You.

So How Are You
Get the fuck over it!
Earth our Jewel in the sky.
Having to fill in the blanks ~
How do I know what's happening?
Live from the heart
blazing in their Cosmic kisses and blisses to the end
You're a selfish, deceitful, dishonest person to me.

*

I Am Another Yourself
*Adopting a Sensory Mind-Field * In Lake chad*
Fucking with a live volcano, bringing Expansion!
"I'll be back on the razzle"
Coming from the source of Life.....
She's lost in not so blissful ignorance!
Being in the heart with bad brain, Neti neti.

*

'Vous êtes en relation avec un répondeur téléphonique'
Naturally trippy, who was a hippy, who is a hippy
who is not a hippy and who will be a hippy?
'No Blacks, No Irish, No Dogs, No Babies,
No Europeans, No Muslims, No Asians,
*No Insane Humans * No Egobots too!'*

*

Planet Consciousness
Bodhisattva motivation? Helping people to Total Acceptance...
Invitation, even in your biggest nightmare... beautiful Cancer!
You need Love medicine
Not real in the mind, simulated as the future or past ~
Only experience, Instantly, immediate, Present Space.
Behaviour from living out their pre-conditioned mental state.
Intention... past Memories, future Imagination, all Illusions.
Ego > 'I AM MY THOUGHTS' Fears and Anxieties of loss.
*I AM * BEING HERE * Attention; As it really, really Is NOW.*

<u>Earthquakes -Tax Free # Heavens.</u>
"There's mushrooms in every forest of the World"
The ground is moving all the time, Psychedelic Lotus.
The Planet is Non-Stop, breaks the normal fuzzy Logic,
Conditioning ~ Paradigm shifting outside the inter-net.
"Terminate the rogue drone, clone for clear energy.
Psycho-Robotics, hybrid females come to spawn.
"If your magic doesn't work what can you do?"
Decloaking, to become visible again, turning off a cloaking device.
To believe or not to believe; African slaves chanting to their Gods.
16-year-old with a Kalashnikov and Qat, total urban tribal!
You with another man's boot on your back.
It's about humiliation; I'm a hippie not in the human traffic business.
Cruising off the Moons of Neptune; hybrid babies in Prison jackets.
Success depended on Aphrodite's Sacred birth and Vision Quests.
"If you want it perfect, get a Print." "From the beginning is Vibration"
"What am I doing here, am I contributing to this devastation?"
What's it like to be in the middle of an eruption? Ask Brahma.
Absolutely, It's Give & Take ~ her favourite Yatra
*

<u>Beyond Heaven and Hell</u>
'Good Christian girls don't get pregnant ~
if they get raped'. Shattering all my reflections.
Instant Karma, the aim is to eliminate all debt!
Whatever is happening is coming from the whole,
is Real, is Reality, is being here now in the totality of Life ~
We fall in Love with the Spacesuit, forgetting all about what's
Inside it! Even if we don't understand, accept it for what it is ~
even if it's in her Ego-Syntonic algorithm because it's ALWAYS
CHANGING ~ How do you want to change with it, miracle Baby?
Under that bright light you can't hate or blame anyone else.
You lived that Unique experience of Your-Self.
Diving into multi-streaming Consciousness.

Master, Mistress of the Spice
GCHQ*Fake narratives of MK. Ultra-Complicity.
'Shot them all, dead in Canary Wharf' E. London.
One man's Terrorist is another man's Stunt actor.
Emptied the bullion vaults, all the rest is a sideshow!
It looks grim because they should all be f…king arrested.
Ask how the Mossad knew about it in advance? "It's a plane!"
Remotely controlled, transmuting into exploding Thermite dust.

*

Energy of Life ~ I am not just this body.
A Form to carry the Soul, Nature is Not for fucking - Fracking!
If you can recognise the source, not exploiting it as a resource.
Use the complete loss of Ego to Open your perception ~
'Death is just the loss of the Personal, Illusional projection'
Suffering is limiting the Unlimited, mind-based Conditionality.
Animals are Life based.

*

Cherry Boy
A paedophile, special kind of beast to do that!
And Kissangore started mass-murdering people.
He got away with genocide, this satanic Icon.
And she might look like a frail old granny
but she's an interbred-reptile monster!
They don't know, strange, isn't it?
Totally rude and disrespectful.
Is it why people idolise her?

*

Super Jammmy
Let's go to the Love Hotel.
Give her the password ~
Breathless, it's been Epic!
Nice to suit yourself ~ Happy.
He had 8 Cambodian girlfriends.
Living the dream * simultaneously

<u>Lighting for Liberation</u>
When you're walking down the street with your own jurisdiction.
The copper doesn't have any rights to do fuck all!
You are the head of a State of Natural Law.
'If you don't say NO, it's consent!'
All the bad boys are in bed.....
Who's motivated by religious hatred?
30% of the land's destroyed by Agent Orange, the rest napalmed!
After bombing Hanoi to bits and poisoning Ho Chi Minh's family,
going through the Valley of the shadow of death
did they get Liberated…
*

<u>Can't see their faces</u>
Who was it who decided to murder John Lennon?
Type, 'CIA. Assassin' into google, see what comes up!
Depends if you're walkin' around, fixated in your dream.
Fulfilling beautiful reality, took him to Intensive nursing.
It's nice to be nice, did God answer your prayers?
Money greed is the greatest mire of our times ~
You wake up in the morning and you're fucked!
Defend your people and the environment.
In the Factory of the World ~ We are minimal-Tao
*

<u>Full Sunshine</u>
Artists, they look for the beauty.
'Free Time is a real luxury...'
Kali destroys duality....
looking at things relatively.
'Those that are wise lament neither for the living nor the dead'
"What do I want to see when I open my door?"
Krishna always surrounded by milkmaids
Having a big smile on your face ~
Follow your dhamma, it's all me.
The entire Universe.

The Mafia Is the Ego
A conceptual Bird on a wire ~
Not seeing it, named it a 'Tree'
(When it's ALL a MYSTERY)
to the self-seeking Mad-Mind.
There is No duality - No beginning or end!
*Its Totality * IS Now * keep smiling Inside.*
*

Hip-noetic-Magic
'The only way to Stop Unconsciousness is to become Conscious'
And God created the Rainbow ~ it's damned heresy they say...
Indoctrinated, they'll believe anything that's made up.
Fed with fake news and distorted perceptions of Life
Mind Controls, brainwashing, Auto-suggestion!
Pointing at the Kingdom of Heaven Inside You.
*

Gluten Intolerance Putin
Being Poisoned by something, undetectable,
Polonium-21 preservatives in the Corn Flakes.
Something is going on, winding kids up on medication.
Food for Thought, Venom in the nano-chips and pot of tea.
What to do in Phnom Penh with the Khmer Rouge about?
Eating grasshoppers, frogs, snakes and Cockroaches...
It's RAW WAR deciding who lives or dies!
Welcome, bienvenue to the Killing Fields.
*

Experiencing It
Thinking that you Know all Existentially ~
Where is the Hidden hand lurking tonight?
"We're all Lab rats"
'You can take a horse to water but can't make it shit'
The Magic wand of Universal Studios, Hollywood's wagging dog.
Just a Mirage of Mental-content not the Power of Now, signposts.
Embracing Silence's Golden Emptiness

Poisoning the Crop
Luddites protecting the land ~
Covered in Toxicity... Mind & body
'The Biology of Belief'
All knowledge is flawed in the brain.
What is the Mind-set of a human cell?
Making new genes.... the Totality of One.
Your skin reacting to Fear or Love's perceptions.
Life's chemicals sensing the Universal intelligence.
Receptors feeling 10 trillion neurons going off!
It's an absolute, Unknown Mystery
Not calling a bird by any name.
*

White sugar is hell for your pancreas
Try some pink Himalayan salt crystals.
Thinking critically between the lines...
How can they justify all that Suffering?
Cambodia's curse, where's brother No 1?
He was a history teacher before he became a psychopath.
All from the same intellectual school of maniacs.
Embryonic matter full of stem cells in my soup.
There's enough money to pay everyone to live.
*

'Lighting Up Damascus!'
80% of Psychedelic soldiers wanted to Quit! War that is!
Changed to using a new generation of Dolphin Guided Missiles!
She's not letting someone take something from her without a fight!
Welcome to the rainbow of the Moslem brotherhood, aligned insurgents,
Army of Conquest, Grandsons of the Prophet, the foreign volunteers ~
extremist Jihadists, Saudis, Qataris, Emiratis, Turks etc. being sponsors
private funders, donors, hedge fund managers at Prism, CIA & Mossad.
Islamists, ideologues, nationalists, Free Syrian Army of Daesh psychos.
Gift of 120 tons of explosives and weapons from the Princely Sultan ~
Ghoutra, great chemical massacre, guilty of atrocities against humanity!

The sun of our heart
A touchdown, 'bound is describable, unbound is indescribable'.
This is one struggle too many, in this seemingly ignorant Corrupt,
'Bakshish Rules' office they call the world, but as you know so well
from your writing, photos, travels and experiences that there are so
many other realms and to maintain the highest conscious, not to be
attached to the suffering caused by these crazy, Tyrants in Power!
'One more step to prove you're human'
*

How the Fuck did they do it?
Life * is the Totality * coming from the Whole so whatever
exists is ~ 'Reality' because it exists here now completely.
It has nothing to do with me effecting the Universe.
We are a lake reflecting, we are integrated in its flow ~
The most perfect place in the world.
"You cannot feel sad in a house with kittens!"
*

Transmigrating B-21 Raider
Love Is Trusting Yourself * A fact…
She's got the same 'I' pod as the Dalai Lama.
Question… 'How do I measure happiness?'
Innocence not Ignorance is bliss*...*
Why do it if you can get someone else to do it?
"He'll always make me a nice chillum"
Bought a flying carpet in Afghanistan.
*

Varanasi Massage
Too much money to spend...
'If you pay peanuts you get monkeys'
A reality check when the lights go out...
PEACE IS LOVE * Meditation * be who you are.
Is Life * is now * is the Totality * One is All * Om
so everything is becoming ~ as essentially it is

*PSY*CHI*
Go in the Trance ~
Shine out in the light
*

Psychos own the Asylum
Where is the invisible man or woman or elemental, angelic ones
when you need them? Have you looked in the Paradise Papers?
This is but one example, where are those with the responsibility
and authority to expose and bring to Justice those criminals
perpetrating violence and horrors against innocent people
and nature, obviously, they do not exist! A bunch of mad,
conquering, tyrannical despots on the rampage again!
'Resolution*Revolution, no minimum wage offshore!'
Evolution is embracing Love, not Sociopaths
Tendencies of empathies, try your best.
*

Love Naturalism
The female's way of life ~
No male logic, more emotional!
Truly Integrating Heart and Mind.
Psycho distortions in Mirror images.
How much real Information is there?
Don't believe anything, be intrinsic ~
How much honest feeling exists within?
A simple sign from the one you are Loving.
*

Lucifer's Cream
Reality TV shows; You can't make this up but we do, always.
And when civilians were 'accidently' blown to smithereens!
"Take us straight to Mossad Headquarters, in Jerusalem!"
Chelsea Manning, Wikileaks exposing their blood thirst!
"I don't want 'collateral damage' as my cause of death!"
On a tombstone, Be Free or Die; Shalom, Inshallah, Om

Pineal * Gland
Degenerated egoism, forgot how to use it...
Try tuning ~ you into Higher Consciousness.
Lens for focusing light, not any illusion * delusion of
bipolarity melting, a bare reality of narcissistic kissing.
Travelling Ups and downs ~ what do you want again!
You're on the Plateau of Intuition ~
The most Important, change is there.
We breathe Prana ~ higher Vibrations
how we see Consciousness flowing ~
Bringing Heaven and Earth Together
*

Shukriya * Born a Slave!
Not officially abolished in Morocco.
Slave married a Slave, "no, do I?"
They are scholars from Timbuktu.
Committed to the begging bowl ~
One camel can feed 300 at a party.
Nature coming into your Mind-fields ~
What is this karmic embedded Id*entity?
Lost my Memory, kept an insight of reality.
*

Sunshine Trips Bless Bliss
Tree of War, a hail of bullets! "This is Johnnie's severed head!"
"The ubiquitous terrorists still haven't left the building yet"
Empire Sociopath Vibe, PSY-OPS, raising its Ugly head.
Invasion of your Privacy; Willkommen meine Freundin.
"How much blood have they got on their hands?"
All in their Uniforms, holding M16's… a Live Feed.
Shooting at the Star constellation of Totalitarianism.
"Let's go to the Glowworm Grotto darling"
Bring the secret in the heart of inner Love.

Mars Attack on Murderous Bedlam!
'Your hull's all that's between you and the deep blue sea'
Prime Minister of a State of National Insanity, Insecurity.
"Air Force One has just landed in Israel."
Being preoccupied with the Chief Inquisitor!
Saluting the Psychopathic, King Herod's hybrid; tyrants
at your front gate, swords ready for the next massacre!
The Power at the Top is really where It doesn't belong!
Free Flowing, cutting off the snake's head of Lucifer!
What is a revolution?
*

Bon Voyance Auras
Pussy in ecstasy, she Loves that big Priapus phallus!
Look at her smiling face between my knees.
*Crystal gazing * Surrender and be Free.*
Ask any Greek or Roman poet ~
who has witnessed the cherry Goddess.
Mythological faeries, nymphs, nereids,
translucent Orbs come to play with you.
Sleeping with Angels' ~ blissful Tulips.
Sitting peacefully in her water garden.
Gazing into adoring Lotus eyes ~
Happy family is the best of my life.
*

Polyamorous Petroglyphs
Nefelibata, "a cloud walker, one who lives in the cloud
of their own imagination or dreams, or one who does
not abide by the precepts of society, literature, or art;
an unconventional, unorthodox person." Not a Sociopath…
Just another projection, be Conscious; going beyond, beyond.
Red lines in the soft red snow, Shiva valley not Silicon Valley.
"Empty your mind, be formless. shapeless, like water ~"
Bruce Lee.

<u>Resonating Dimensions</u>
Pussy willows beside a fluorescent, magical, faerie pool.
It means we're taking it one day at a time ~
"Regular as clockwork, cuppa tea and a shit,
most people are like that, ain't they?
"An average 4 out of 10 will participate in the stoning!"
"The lesser of two evils is still evil mate, look at the Caliphate"
*

<u>Officially Sunflares blowin' the Fuse.</u>
Unnaturally, they're taking us over ARTIFICIALLY-ID.
"We're all part of it mate, don't go to Chandi Chowk.
Overwhelmed by it, NWO. it's all a bit of a big mess.
'It's Not Thinking what you can get next
but FEELING what You can Give ~
Experiencing breath & being here.
S I M P L E * S M I L E S
The Miracle that you can be
A L I V E * L I F E * F R E E
And walk easy down the street
*

<u>Natural * Creation</u>
Whole * No Separation
'It's FREE FORM'
TRANS * PARENT
Vox angelica in her light summer dress.
'Everyone is as Holy as the next or not...
Not them, it's their involuntary Sociopathology.
How unconsciously did you treat your children?
Everybody's good when being in the Present moment.
We leave no trace ~ "I was at the Heartbreak Motel"
"Darling take that bone out of your nose,
do you think you're in a primitive tribe?"

POD SWITCH

Beautiful Vibe, how are you growing in Intuition Delphine?
Following stepping stones, tones of Emoto's liquid crystals
across the pink Lotus pond of Ten Thousand Opening Petals ~
Is there such a thing as legal, Holy War? Only if you serve Mammon!
'Your Program is on Normal for You, to someone else it's Not Normal'.
Red Cloud watching black clouds pass overhead along the Peace river
Sociopathy means you can deny; allow the slaughter of all Innocents.
Ego-syntonically, your feelings only support your own survival needs!
*

Arabian Satyrs dangling at the end of a rope.

Torture, sorry, 'Enhanced Stress Techniques' in dark Chambers!
Flagellation below an Oval Room. 'Disappeared' after school.
Where? Not for the sketching of irreconcilable, joyous nudes.
Does one think something should be done father?
* Fluorescent yellow fireballs * pinned to her eyes ~
"I feel very Free at the moment" ~ gone out of my Mind!
Old Lion King, Predator of the jungle, "out of business."
Electronic tagged, determining your access to ~ reality!
*

On the Top Stoned

"I Love bare leg, I'd eat that to death mate,
I'm goin' to slither ~ up there and get you!"
Be Yourself; Why? Be Whoever You want to be ~
No meta-data mining, rattling, holding you on track.
Where and when is the Fertility time?
*

Coitus' Shanti Honey

Panspermia * Coddiwomple * Wisdom written by an Unknown…
'The happiest people don't always have the best of everything
THEY JUST MAKE THE BEST OF EVERYTHING THEY HAVE'
Fungo * Magico, Paradise is instantaneous Consciousness ~
A blissful moment in the ever-changing state of Space
Cosmic Revolution

'Omnia vincit amora' * 'Omnia mutantur nos et mutamur illis'
Stopping the Pendulum ~ Opening up, not Political Correctness.
Monkeys from space ~ don't have Souls, crime on every corner.
Square mile, City of London, heartless chakra of the Universe?
Living in a Gated country, an Island Prison, Custodial services!
Security extremely necessary - Your own Protection; Guarded!
Keeping us all in or them all out, Is there any Real difference?
Mind Expansion or Consciousness Expansion of Perception?
Suppression, repression, obsession, oppression, depression.
Sad old refrain ~ can't take Suffering without any empathy!
That's exhibit **A**; What are you Really doing about Darfur?
A bully in every classroom, nursery, every refugee camp!
Started making art myself ~ streaming of consciousness
_*_

Mr. Sugar Cube & Miss Aromatic Temptation
'We have selected hot housewives, 10 miles within your location'
Big Clit, Creampie, music Compilation, 3 married women in bed.
Going down to the heart and switching it off for good!
Over-riding it with a concept of your abstract Mind ~
What do I feel in practice? Your heart's a quiet place.
Something's coming through, we're imitating, initiating.
'I'm my self-Identity, program' Unplugged, the way I think.
Playing with your own imagination at the end of the process.
Stop doing what you're told and do some critical thinking ~
Gotta keep body and soul together in this World of Space.
A mental-movement too far down the road.
I've let it all go *now* you're where you are ~
Secret Psychedelic-head, you're touching Truth.
"We are the Universe, I've seen so many little bits"
Writing a love poem, condensing energy into Infinity.

<u>Unity for Unity's Sake Is a Round Line</u>
Pictures of expectation ~ No possessions or Yes Sir!
Each being makes their own Involution ~ re*evolution.
Living, sharing Magical Rainbows and Solar eclipses ~
Pain in confusion, worry doesn't help, only accentuates.
Not Trusting, that's what Spinning Propaganda's about.
Giving our energy to the Governors of Fear, not going ~
through the star gates at the end of your road dear. And
Ma Kali brings you beyond time ~ bring it on; Full Power!
Goddess Shakti enshrining Shiva's blossoming flower.
I Love that little saxophone's, engorging, golden tune.
Staying in eternity everything is meditation.
No need to force the seeds of life
in the heart of the infinite galaxy.
*
<u>Not a Drop - Stop!</u>
Where you gonna get your water today?
No need of resistance from the Mind ~
Against the natural flow ~ the momental.
Jumping into the Florien belt of Love bells
with Mayan worshippers of Suns and Moons.
Making the circle round ~ Spiralling Cosmic Kells.
Spent a season with Shanti Baba at a trance party.
Multi-dimensionality, sparks contact into human forms ~
going Inside the poles, frictional Love, the Psychic Wars.
LSD. fire moths don't need magic plasma or laser beams,
going against the grain. Sai Baba called me in my dreams.
Floating in swirling currents at a natural spring's pools of Love.
Imprinting, reflections glinting * living the most potential energy.
Learning Freedom in my Dreamboat World

I'll do some Meditation after I've made the wall Higher.
Jumped the Gun - and Shot Your Self in the foot!
Madrigal, "I am going mad"
"Myths expressing your mentality"
Met a nixie, a pixie, a Rabbi, sorry rabbit,
by the banks of ~ Affinity with the Divine.
Thanks for reminding me * Love Conquers All*.
'All things change, and we change with them'
*Love Is All * Light * no light * Star bright*
*

My Corps * Oil Protocol

The Queen rules as God's agent under Natural law.
It's a Crime only for breaking the law, not a statute…
I'm not refusing to give my DNA. but it costs $2 million!
'90% of people in US's jails are there voluntarily'
A Public servant's oath is to uphold the Law ~
to protect my rights, ensure not trespassed.
We're not in Business under the Law Society
that's commercial; taking on my own Authority!
You can have an opinion but here is the evidence…
Psy-warfare, Geo-engineering being fabricated somewhere.
Made an ionosphere bubble; replacing it with something new.
*

3D Depth Standard

And this randomness of two people sharing a Crystal.
Less regulations and the people are less regulated too.
You really never know; I try to bring out the best in people.
Not a recipe for Paranoia; know we are the Power, it's simple.
About Awareness >conditioning's not <Omniscient Education.
Is it your problem that somebody else has a f…king problem?
It's never too late for a tiniest bit of empathy sweetheart….

<u>Unelected, Undemocratic, Monarchic Evil Forces</u>
Manic, her body pumped full of Embalming fluids ~
Mysteriously Vanished; Quest of keeping Alive!
'Diane was unstable, that was their problem!'
They had her reproductive organs removed ~
Believing Moslems would enter the Royal blood lineage ~
'Dividing and Conquering, invading, liberating their wealth!'
it's all a hoax, until you get the shock and awe of a drone
sending you Hellfire missiles, then it's collateral damage!
Crimes Against Humanity they should all be Locked up,
judged, then sent back to the Devil! But they're allowed
to escape any prosecution, these leading psychopaths.

*

*<u>"You are Dead * We are in Heaven"</u>*
Psy*trance is for dancing, it puts me in a good mood.
Stepping outside the Matrix for Real, from Your Mind.
"I'm in my own jurisdiction even if I'm shagging!"
"I don't wanna do anybody out of anything"
"I'm on my own I can do anything I want"
Don't have to answer to Mr. Mrs. Anybody.
Wearing the hat of my own Person, mine!
FREE to do whatever you want, desire.
A Big Illusion, actually in Brahma land.
Let's have a Shiva Valley Party!

*

<u>Candle Rays</u>
Fell into the pit ~
of selfish, greedy ego…
Dark, full of poisonous vipers.
Tried some romantic, sociopathy tragedy.
Transcended it, sharing in some more Solar Power
Into light beams ~ non-duality, evolutionary spectrum.
Going around a wormhole in radiant consciousness

How do they get away with it?
YOU ~ the main thing is what's your journey in Life?
You can spend as much as you want, to get what you want.
We've heard the whispers of Total Control - nothing in the News.
Waiting for the mainstream event, leading to Big Banging Brother.
A figure of their creative Accountants' Imagination!
She's never got enough, give her some more.
They seem to be taking it without any regard.
Everybody Loves the Monarch's propaganda.
But these people are royally taking the Piss!
*

Switch it Off
Facially recognised from 600ft; and Insider trading, the smoking gun?
Lying on the floor laughing her head off ~ held by the Palace guard!
'They had to improve a design that was perfect' as happy as can be.
Termination of #6 ~ why would you want that on your conscience?
Robbery by Stealth, Austerity, "I refuse to drink it", keep on going ~
They're not tellin' 'em any time soon about the deception, the heist!
You gotta look after me, I got rights, for public servants to protect…
They want everybody doing what they're told; a dystopian theme park!
'None so blind as those who won't see.' Here is the Christmas twitter.
Loving their Royal, Mass hypnosis, Soap Opera, Trooping the Colour.
Pomp and Ceremony, "It's not what you see and think, it's how you feel
or not, as a serf, inferior subject of an elite's superior, Imperial Crown"
*

Sunni Royal Fakes - FFS!
Saudi Arabia, Qatar $upplying the means to target the Shia's in Syria!
II is a Sunni operation working with devilish Zions to destroy the Shia.
Mass immigration strategy, diluting national cultural identity of Europe ~
so easier for Globalists to Control and they took it hook, line and sinker!
The Shia say it's all about their bloke called Ali; owned by Nothingness.
"We are the people chosen by the One God; apparently not mate!"
Baba BOOM!

122

Fakery, Frippery of Grovelling Lackeys
What is it Heaven or Hell; Love and hate?
Dying in your dreams and never waking up ~
Knowing when the game's up, like an old elephant.
God's given right is to protect anything, even foxes!
Councillors of the Local Authority wanna be Insiders.
"I want what they're havin' and fuck the rest of you!"
*

Gagging Orders
Her letters were redacted, biased, censored the evidence, curfew!
She's in pieces; I spend money on making my life easy, really good.
I don't wanna do anything now;
I don't believe in what anybody says anymore!
My blood is boiling, I'm into escapism that's all.
"You can play with me if you want."
I had a good time, that's the bottom line; is it? "I'm happy."
"I've been in some blocks of flats where they have flowers
on every windowsill and your dad's growing a bit of weed.
"Wasn't that the day I got busted?"
*

A very big drop down
Sitting in a café reading my book.
A girl sat down and gave me a sachet of Viagra.
And when I turned around she just smiled ~
If I don't do it now how will I ever know?
A process of renewal, if I want something
I get it, otherwise a load of stress, thinkin' 'bout it!
*

Processing a Sort of Evolution in Space
There are ripples in the lake ~ who knows the whole story, Excalibur?
Your cells can only absorb so much then give it back to the Universe.
Unless you're tripping, then you get the nano-detail ~ You get it Raw!
It looks like distortion; it's everything really, not cleaning it out ~
Feeling groovy, brain's filtering 11 million signals per second

Different Food
She likes Speedy balls,
She likes 'Wonderland!'
*She gets her energy from it * She likes coke too for her ego!*
Why persecute her, a tragic abuse of the Innocent victim?
"I never feel like doing bad on good acid"
*Using Up All Your tokens * Receptors.*
*Psy*stems and roots of a Bodhisattva*
*

SHIVA ENERGY CONTINUOM
Changes of Polarity, teaching me to be here now.
There's a common program for everything, XYZ-
What you lookin' at, what you paying attention to?
You're not lookin' at yourself, it's all a big distraction.
Our mind needs duality, reactions, cause and effect.
We're flying easily brainwashed; Observe your Mind.
You'll all want something else in 2 secs. or 2 minutes!
Shut up and play with your I'ego, switch off the default!
Gotta remember it's about you, your energy, your spirit.
Everything's been Programmed. We've always been slaves!
Everything's a stepping stone, you become something ~
then you unbecome it; let's go look at the sunset darling.
*

Laugh out Loud * Transcend
They're addicted to their own thoughts, obsessively, OCD!
Started hating everybody, negative, mental constructions.
Precious that you don't know things, even past and future.
Distraction going to enforce a sense of Self. Go work it out!
Why does my mind wander? I am right ^ You are wrong!
This whole thing, look within my mind-set's working ego.
That's where God and the Devil are.
Deal with it by Switching it OFF!

<u>Your Hysterical Eugenics</u>
Ridlin, people with bullets, "I wanna wake up!"
"They can't lock you up if you're free inside"
'Don't ever take drugs that disagree with you ~'
Surrounded by people who believe in the bullshitting.
Can't put your child in school without being vaccinated!
You are the magic not the place, being happy everywhere.
I want to be sad, I want to be happy, I changed my mind…
"Everybody said that it was a regular beheading!"
Taking advantage of the divine Trust.
*

<u>Metaphor of the Cave</u>
Peter Pan Shaman in my Chrysanthemum garden ~
He saved her from a time of madness; got no thanks!
Conscious butterfly and stung by a pollinating bumble bee.
The treachery of a caress, no heart, no feelings, Narcissus.
Who is doing all this abusing today of our innocent children?
Psychic wars, the explosion occurred at a pop concert!
Chained gates, the enemy is inside, demon software ~
Anatomy of a great deception, uninterruptible autopilot.
"The whole point of the Welfare state is that we all
Protect each other, we're all protected by each other"
La Place du Miroir, Love is a gift; it's not self-evident.
A direct connection with Pachamama, Trusting in Life ~
Hand in hand, vibrating, fluttering softly on warm breezes
*

<u>Simple, came for the Up*Loading, the Inspirational</u>
not the down-loading, want some free Loving baby?
Forever on a come down, leaving in a bad mood.
"I wouldn't lick it!" Sucking it dry as a sour grape.
Meditation, 'be who you are' ~ in the stillness
being in the trance flow, forget all the rest.
'The wealthiest man is a free time*man'
Straw in his trousers, free as a gypsy

Elite Terrorism's Not Nature.

'Legalised', special activities 'Enhanced Interrogation!'
'Zionists don't believe in miracles', an anti-Semite said.
POV still hated for killing Jesus… Need a Serotonin refill...
The World stinks Baba, the World needs a monster enema!
"If I could take a million people with me, I'd blow myself up!"
Human greed, all it is. Suffering for what man does to man!
Look at the tyranny happening over at North Dakota pipeline.
Where's Barbara Streisand when you need her input mate?
Nothing stranger than folk, used to dealing with all the angels.
*Try Astral projection * Living more in the now, raising seeds*

*

Sea * Shells

She sells micro-bikinis on the seashore ~
Cunctipotent, metaphor for sublime, Heavenly.
"I don't believe in Santa Cause any more Baba"
A Selfish, heartless, ignorant, lost, black magic kunst.
No fear, you get up there, something about Confidence
not a shattering self-identity, scared of your own shadow!
She put her fingers all over it, Shiva ling in a crystal Temple.
What Do You want? Not giving it any more attention!
Old enough to have tantrums, they came out of a cage!
Bought them at the Friday, ordained, slave market.

*

Total Relaxation

Grab those tits, squeeze those puffy nipples ~
Auric fingertip on her throbbing, engorged clit!
Tongue on her tongue, rub it up and down!
Are you ready ~ Hot and sweaty
Hard and harder.
She loves to suck a Big fat cock mate!
Harder and harder, again, again, again!
She sucks like an uncontrollable sociopath
bitch, she fucks like a dirty Queen.

<u>Cosmic Energy Grove</u>
"I was in Love first"
Fuck the System…
I feel empowered, understanding ~
why I'm getting screwed every day.
"It's not Rocket science!"
Spread the Love
*

<u>We'll be on a Hit-list Baba</u>
Under the Vatican is a central pillar of Satanism.
The local council is now a Totalitarian Authority,
controlling of the mass-media consciousness.
Not everybody's a mad cunt in this world,
do you have a bullet proof vehicle and mercenaries?
It's not what you think, it's how you FEEL (In your heart).
You're the Real world, sharing with people what's goin' on.
You gotta integrate ~ It's that simple
*

<u>He Loves It</u>
'Beer makes life better'
She just fucked him off
because she's tired of it ~
and she told him, 'You don't exist anymore!'
A gram a day and they're fuckin' for a druggin'
or druggin' for a fuckin'. Don't blow up the rat!
"The smack is here, crack is on the way" - met in Rehab.
MDMA & Viagra, "Oh no, give us some more and more!"
A World of Entertainment, girls attacking a big fat Cock!
*

<u>Dissolving Beingness</u>
Prana ~ concentration on the changing breath.
Conscious of the Matrix-mind's illusion of thought.
*Wandering through your Multi*verses…*
It's always there totally

127

<u>Self-Possessed - Greedy Social Crimes</u>
How many Palaces do you need? Try Organic, permaculture working!
The government's tellin' yu one thing and doing exactly the opposite!
Devising a Punitive tax system while all theirs is offshore, PM et al!
Free speech, maybe you can but who does? All craving Insiders...
Who is giving and taking, caring, sharing in the energetic vibe?
Feeling the lingam's deeper penetration ~ how much for a kiss?

*

<u>Alchemistic Magical Process * Opening a Shell</u>
Psychedelics * to realise * Open the Mind-set ~
Transmutation of matter, finding a Universal elixir.
High cheeks spreading, that's always the excuse...
"don't bogart that joint my friend pass it over to me"
Spliff's not finished! It's not a crime against humanity!
When someone you Love denies your very existence!
Another illusion, betrayal of your deepest attachments!
Want some PTS? Keep it simple, turning everyone on ~

*

<u>WHY?</u>
I can't Stop loving you!
I have to accept that ~
Inside We Love You
Why not, why Stop?
Changing is infinitely
In eternal Love Space

*

<u>Betrayed and Denied-Dragonnade</u>
Enslaved ~ "Maybe we could buy some time Master?"
"I can't help but wonder, mais êtes vous le Roi-Soleil?"
Is it transhuman, corgis, running the Palace Theatre?
The mind is chatter, nonstop chattering, a hologram ~
'Genki' - Chi in your roots, tested in a Faraday cage.
Mind ~ leave the world outside, it's getting insane!
Rainbow fractal vibrations spin inside kaleidoscopes

<u>A Labour of Love</u>
CREATING WO/MAN WITH/OUT HUMANITY!
"If you want to become a Fearless traveller..."
'Be all that you can be', what is it? An Artificial cloud!
Toxic, stealing your time in a Panasonic, electric house.
Nirvana seeker of the Truth dimension, Love it all Darshan.
Happy Satsang, the key to me and super Bhakti, pure devotion.
'War on fear, war on drugs, they don't want people being happy'
Missing the moment ~ getting wasted, paranoid contravention.
It depends how much in spirit you are, making you shine inside.
"Beautiful to be pregnant ~ the sky is super gorgeous today."
*

<u>FREE TO SHARE</u>
Shinto ~ time is God, God is Now, time is ~
"I dance to Peace and Love for all humanity"
Respect the Nation, your tribe, but Free Camping, free reservation...
Communicating with each other, something we can all agree on or not?
Someone has to share (and care), No one really Knows ~ relativity
Ganja skies, living in a Psy*trance, tribal village by Bom Shanka lake.
'One person's phantasm is another person's reality, n'est pas, cherie?'
*

<u>His last Act</u>
Signing on the dotted line… Hari Kiri Insurance!
Honour for his family, the final, live sacrifice!
Crazy mentality, desperate in Ginza....
Outside a noodle shop...   broken!
SMASHED INTO A MILLION PIECES.
It's a casino; no one wins in a casino...
You can't say No; tempting, too much needy greed.
Public Indecency, being prosecuted... for 'Exposure'
Chasing a young hippy Geishabot in Tokyo; tattoos
on her legs, a ring in her clit ~ lustrous silvery lips.

Fuck those bastardos
No one wants to be a human sacrifice ~
Filleting children's hearts atop a diamond pyramid!
Mermaids are swimming, in the light of the setting Sun.
'Sattva' ~ Being existence, the true quality of goodness.
Nothing to prove to my loving and compassionate divinity.
It's all a factory, slave mentality; who's afraid of the Gestapo?
Our intimacy, whose responsibility is this Baby?
"I burst into tears, it was beautiful and wonderful"
Giving birth around a campfire ~ contact with a human being!
"As a guide I've been to the summit of many mountains and back"
*
Shanti Weed Menu
*Welcome to Goa * a good place to go Mad!*
"Another one who doesn't want to be Happy"
"I have difficulty standing in a line of Obsessions"
"Anyone want some therapeutic Opium?" "Changa?"
*Micro-dose Acid for Sale * LSD; advertised on his T shirt ~*
CBD. easy medicine; for everything that's wrong with you!
Channelling on drugs ~ an Infinite array
*
A Police State by Design
"Travelling makes your heart stronger."
"Traveller needs courage, or you die."
"I go with good Intentions." Not swarms of drones.
Why doesn't the mainstream media tell the truth?
Always following the money to the guilty cabal.
Feeding from the bottom up, feeding oxygenator.
In a Peace garden there are no smart weapons!
Keeps on producing pro-bacteria, which saves.
*Crimes Against Humanity*Crimes Against Earth.*
More Ecocide, 'War Is Not Beautiful'. Radish is...
"Mosquito leave me in peace and it's all ok; bight
me, I'll Zap you!" "And what are you after now?"

Benign * be now
You just have to listen; you know everything...
Nakedness ~ Nothing to hide, Cosmic nudity.
Nature, nothing where you gotta think about it.
He never got over her ~ Oh Fuck!
Pura vida, our future is naturalism ~
Happy for no other reason ~ Love All.
On the healthy psychedelic side of life.
"I live like that in my garden"
Sunshine is good, dancing for pleasure
_*_

Rustic Bohemian
"Love is the best" ~ "For sure!"
'Someone has to share ~ sharing is scaring
for some; another one who can't be happy.
Meditation without the Pain…
if your mind-body's not in the way.
A sensible micro*dose for breakfast!
_*_

Yeah, I'll have a drop!
They're taking Buddha's image in Vain.
Don't Idolise any object ~ 'It is Not me'
Don't worship, he didn't ask for anything…
People just gave him things; what's it all mean?
Poetry read out in court Judge ~ I've had that honour!
Going to the ends of the World for someone you Love.
Back and forth ~ everyone's doing Qi Gong in the park
_*_

Mind the Nature
Everyone's Loved Up ~ Going all night…
Expanding Universe, dancing is contagious.
Lila * Cosmos is seen as the Divine play…
A head start, the window of opportunity
for the fastest sperm ~

Tantric Purusha
"NO-NO-NO ~ You can't touch me!"
Saying Yes, always to Shiva Shakti.
'Can't beat 'em, might as well join 'em!
ENJOY THE DAY
The Cosmic Spirit ~ the Eternal Nature.
Tattva ~ the True essence; Satya, Truth.
*

Growing * Flowers
I don't do it for the money ~ being in touch.
He married a famous bee-keeper's daughter.
They're people who were there for me and I blessed them.
She looked me in the eyes ~ is it true?
*

The Eccentric Maitre d'
Going up inside, Dragonfly 44's galactic array ~
Let's have a night-out in Torremolinos... You know,
at the end, something's going to go badly wrong!
Napalm 'em for now, gas the biological material!
Bight you bad, scratch you deep...
*

I Read Jungle Book
You can't reprimand a horse for being a horse or a kid for being a kid.
Pantomime, deep state's program in existence, before Jesus and co.
No foreigners welcome! Escape ain't cheap. Hit the Nail on the Head!
Excommunicated because God loves us so much, ask Adam and Eva!
If a Tiger raises its head, don't run like fuck, look back; just stay still!
Who is the biggest psychopath? How to recognise 'em? You won't!
"I've always done my best to make it as hippie as possible"
"Everybody's been made, gotta get paid, get laid"
"I've had enough excitement in my life,
not worth so much for that feeling ~
Anti-gravity mantras, levitating megaliths.
Vibrations of flower power

PASSIONATE FLOWER

*Most gorgeous, sweetest, Frangipani petals
in bloom, It's not just an empty Sun Temple ~
Many people scared of Credit default swaps.
Everything's bankrupted, everything's insane!
The money's quantumtatively worthless, but...
Elite's Ponzi Fundamentals are good, he said.
"Usually looking up in the paper sky for UFO's"*

*

Space Oddity

*Only the command needs to be triggered.
Channelling the New Quantum Phoenix.
Giving and Receiving, healing oneself...
forget all those naughty thoughts.
"Get down on your knees and
start scrubbing the floors!"
Keep your focus, right here * now
'Love all and be kind to all because
I live and exist in all' * Sai Baba
An Original Life ~ No Clinging Please.
"I need a Spaceship ready for the Cosmos"
Truly ~ there are humble people here, amongst us.
'You are the Star shooting from the ether in gratitude'
"What if a man conquers the world but loses his soul?"
Mark 8.36. Still in a coma, she really wanted everything!
First time you let go ~ Your breath, Your death, of delusions.
Lost my soul-mate for-ever, here * now; a new, free state of No-Mind.
The perfect Inspiration of music, poetry, healing arts ~ caring is sharing.
Sculptured tree decorations, transformed from machine gun shrapnel!
It was War-waste material, the spoils not a Spiritual overabundance.
Just showing you another way out into the field of this Universe ~
It could be the light, it could be the stones in the river.
Got a print of Diego Rivera's, 'Girl holding white lilies'.
My favourite*

'Judges releasing two suspects in the death of
Scarlet Keating'. Guardian, London, 23/09/2016
One thing of many I remember from this, is that as a member
of the Goa tribal-family living in Anjuna for many years, in my
naïve, 'everyone's nice and high bubble', I was really shocked
to know that there were/are (male) Predators lurking out there,
amidst us stoned hippies, searching for an easy (female)victim
(after an all-night party). They are now mobile, in fast contact
and know that they can get away with it, as statistics on rape
(or as they say in India, 'offending the girl's modesty') prove.
Most rapes go unsolved (this is true in other countries) and
I know the threat is still very prevalent in Goa, as the stories
since suggest. Violent crime has escalated since that moment.
They are cruising around, wired up and capable of anything!
A major turning point for us all. When my teenage daughter
came, over the next two years I was concerned if she was
out at night, especially as she is open and trusting, as we
mostly are to other people and to what they say, ask, in our
'Goa Paradise'. I was at least calmed down, that she had a
mobile phone and hopefully aware enough not to get spiked,
but there is always a vulnerable one! I know for the children
on the beach, who live in Anjuna there is mainly a system of
parental monitoring but we are in Goa to enjoy Freedom too and
that is a delicate balance of forces which now has been undermined.
A similar story of drunken teenagers (Predators) in Delhi 16/12/2012
gang raping an Indian girl on a bus, all premeditated and encouraged
by their frustrated 'Eve teasing' vibe. These males feel invulnerable in
an otherwise closed culture! Unlike in Goa they were swiftly caught!
In Scarlett's case the degree of corruption was incredible and the
panic to offset the blame outside (onto her mother) was monstrous.
It was well organised to preserve the clean image of tourism in Goa
and so protect whoever was really responsible; whoever they were!

*At least the authorities have learnt something, that with today's
Global communications it is now harder to control the reactions
of the press etc. Goa's image suffered and has never recovered,
that is a price local people are still paying. Hopefully it made us
all more aware so that crimes like this wherever they happen will
be dealt with, prevented in the future and the society will let it be
known in their own way that such behaviour will not be allowed.
And without sounding patronising; that young girls need our
protection not our indifference. Knowing that this innocent
girl's murderers escaped 'Justice' is sickening for us all
and we can only hope that India's view, that Karma is
the ultimate justice will prevail and all those guilty will
one day meet Kali! My deepest sympathy goes
to her mother and family * Om Shanti Shanti*

*

White Punk Album

*Pink Adrenalin, Jet black ocean, lapping, softly ~
In All of us * for All of us * feeling * transcendence.
Serotonin sunrise, my lover; the Heart of the Earth.
Ethereal auras from Inner Space, not this rat race...
"Have a Nice Day", completely random, total chaos!
Cut it off at the mouth of the river ~ a Big Deception.
Pure energy accepting everything ~ free expression.
"My life's been major disasters and minor miracles."
A Tomahawk flying right through your living room!
Another perception ~ looking at things differently.
Just ways of thinking, another configured Mind-set.
A million spiders weaving their web around you.
Manifesting these changes into new awareness.
Manifesting all life from our Soul Consciousness ~
Betrayal, slavery or not; a fright, a shock ~ I've had a few!
"Back on the bus or back off the bus, or on both, unknown"
"I'm not a stranger on the dance floor" ~ Infinity matrixed!
I was always free to leave ~ open to the next wave.*

<u>Death Rays * Death Pays</u>
Everyone's on a WIFI. AI. Cloud * Satellite,
NASA, NSA, SPACE X, DARPA; take over!
Let's go see the Royal family down at the Palais.
Skinned by a Sheriff, at the BIS, City of London.
Where are the pollinating bumble bees? fill in
the blanks ~ dead corpses littering the street.
Bathing the entirety of Africa, of the Earth with EMF…
Silicon Valley epicenter, sleepwalking into transhumanism.
Robots, drones, machines, control by Artificial Intelligence?
'Attaching our Mind to a technical sub-reality' ~ Om!
Who is Censoring the true, alternative reality news?
A strand of the web, what is dictating this behavior
and direction of who is at the centre of the web ~
The Research, Development Arm of the Pentagon.
Army Intelligence; who's making these decisions?
In an Android World of Sci-fi now
*

<u>Technological Sub-reality, try a Fractal Hologram</u>
'Nanobots in smart dust connecting into the cloud.
They're high-jacking the human sub/conscious!
Mind-controlling by them running all the programs.
Artificial Intelligence - "What do you want?"
Selling you a super hero personality where
AI. becomes greater than the human mind'
Just a guy who wants to be free
*

<u>Implantable ~ Thinking like a machine</u>
Ending humanity but keeping Transhumans ~
Which cloud is your mind-perception coming from?
I'm having another thought, it's a transgender signal.
Taking us over our emotional field, Tech. it onto the body.
Hi-Tech inside the body, connecting to Control Command
of a human, fractal, holographic Mind ~ "They're still alive!"

*Love is the Lesson * Is it the answer?*
Is it the precious magic of the heart, or is it...
Algorithms, search engines, control, info. manipulation.
WIFI. beamed to the whole Planet, I phone in contact.
Direct connection, WWW. into sub-conscious minds
of me and you and them! Complimentary synchrony ~
brilliant buttercups, cornflowers within Pachamama.
Keeping ahead of the Industrial-brainbotty.
Fecund, natural harmony there to be felt ~
Throbbing of vermillion cowrie, seashells.
Quivering ~ how deep do you wanna go?
I like these tranquil islands in harmony.
Go inside and ask a Cosmic, geometric
tree. Who is thee? Infinite variety, free.
Sunbeams on turquoise, lapping waves.
Yonis glistening in crystal, clear lagoons.
*

Setting the Mind Free ~ Becoming Nothingness
"He who wants to be the Greatest of all will be the servant of all"
Children of the journey, revelations through crystal, white Light.
How does a Mind know anything beyond its mental-boundaries?
*Mindfull * Mindless, to Realise and Discover its own Capacities.*
Can't see its own beauty until we pop through the cloaking veil.
Seeing the Mountain from a distance, the Earth from Space.
*"The Now ~ flying out of the Cocoon * Life Is You're Free"*
"This World is beautiful if you have the heart to feel it"
*

*Multi * Dimensional Feelings * Consciousness*
*It's all about sharing Loving Kindness * May all beings be Happy.*
Mind Clear and Open ~ to be silent, feeling Cosmic Space, metta.
Not Attached to grief anymore, that's a different box. You, putting
your head through a crystallised Rainbow ~ It takes time to wake up
*don't think * Outside the box*

About Sunny Jetsun

Inspired by the sixties, Sunny started traveling the world in 1970. His spiritual journey on the hippie trail to India took him through ~ San Francisco, Los Angeles, London, Amsterdam, Paris, Vancouver, Sidney and Kathmandu to Varanasi. His arrival on the sub-continent ~ was the beginning of writing autobiographical verses capturing his travel experiences, encounters with remarkable people and his quest for self-realization. Combining experimentation with drugs, sex, rock & roll, art, meditation, Love and life in general. Sunny started to open up to a multi-dimensional Universe. He lived the mantra, "Turn on, tune in, drop out" realising Mind's-illusions, inspired by deeper feelings of holistic nature, empathy*energy & Space.

Over four decades Sunny has written and published 30 books of poetry, created over one hundred paintings, traveled the World and considers his masterpiece to be his daughter. He has spent the past sixteen years in Goa, India, inspired by the freedom to experience and idealism of human consciousness.

Sunny Jetsun books and art are available on the web at:
Website: www.sunnyjetsun.com
Facebook: www.facebook.com/sunnyjetsun
Amazon: www.amazon.com/author/sunnyjetsun
Smashwords: www.smashwords.com/profile/view/sunnyjetsun